'Style is a language, a philosophy, an identity.
It is reaction, provocation, rebellion, expression.
It is counterculture. It is subculture. It is
sociopolitical, potent, bold and powerful.
Style Tribes examines how we express our
individuality and our politics by the choices we
make in presenting ourselves to the world. It is
an exploration into the role that style has played
within our culture and a probe into the intent,
the meanings and the weight behind something
we often think of as so frivolous.'

Shirley Manson, Garbage

STYLE
TRIBES

CAROLINE YOUNG

CONTENTS

Introduction

'Fashion is not something that exists in dresses only. Fashion is in the sky, in the street, fashion has to do with ideas, the way we live, what is happening.' Coco Chanel

Style and fashion have long been a means of self-expression, and, often along with music, used as a way to identify with a particular ideology or subculture. It's an act of resistance against the norm, choosing a particular way of life that differs from mainstream culture.

In revolutionary France, the Incroyables and Merveilleuses reacted to the Reign of Terror with decadence and a dandyish, attention-grabbing dress, including wearing a red string around the neck for those who had lost their lives to the guillotine. Scuttlers were late nineteenth-century Manchester gang members who stood apart in their clogs, bell-bottom trousers, silk scarves and crew-cut hair with fringes. An early bohemian feminist movement, the Rational Dress Society, aimed to free women from the confines of cumbersome, constrictive clothing.

It was in the twentieth century that industrialisation, globalisation and modernism brought with them an explosion in these different style tribes, particularly with the great changes in society after the First World War. With emancipation for women, the introduction of child labour laws, education for all and an expanding middle class, there was more time for young adults to enjoy culture, and to consume music and fashion.

Most subcultures are defined by their youthfulness, and this coincided with the introduction of the radio and the gramophone where records could be brought into the home and played at private parties, becoming an indicator of personal taste. Similarly, mass-produced clothing meant that fashion could reach those who wouldn't have previously been able to afford it. Films crossed geographical boundaries by being screened in cinemas around the world, while fashion magazines allowed the latest fashions and trends to be shared far and wide. The flapper style spread out amongst society women and then to working women, who had read of the antics of Flaming Youth in newspapers, and watched Colleen Moore or Clara Bow on screen.

Because records were expensive, most fans would have to save the money to buy the latest release. As a result, they would become more devoted to a particular genre of music. In 1930s Germany there were hot clubs set up across the country, where jazz fans could discuss and listen to the latest records, at a time when jazz was not approved of by the Nazis, and these swing kids dressed in British and American fashions to emulate the source of the music they loved.

African Americans used fashion as a way to show their pride and dignity when their rights and opportunities were limited. Harlem in the 1920s experienced a flourish of self-expression, and by 1940, the zoot suit, with its extravagant structure and shape, acted as a refusal to be subservient. Rudeboys in Jamaica dressed sharp, emulating a wild west fashion, to make a power statement in the midst of rising unemployment as the country moved towards independence from the UK. As Pauline Black, from ska band the Selecter, said: 'Caribbean people don't like wearing other people's cast-offs . . . that's why hip hop artists dress themselves in designer stuff and bling. Black people don't want to look poor, as though they haven't got the money for store-bought clothes.'

It was in the 1950s that the concept of the teenager was first introduced by advertising men, looking for a new way to sell products. Teenagers were a consumerist force and champions of individuality – rather than dressing like their parents, they made the decisions as to what they wanted to buy and wear – and rock and pop music would measure the taste of a person, and what group they belonged to, more than ever before. Mods in particular developed the sense of being part of a secret club, where the 'faces' set the trends with a cool shirt or style of jacket, and had knowledge of the most obscure music.

By the mid-sixties it was young people who were challenging their governments, particularly in the United States, where the hippie movement encouraged young people to 'turn on, tune in, drop out' and to protest against nuclear arms and racism. Gay pride, civil rights and women's liberation also led the way for an increase in subcultures and those that provoked the norm, such as disco, punk and hip hop.

Subcultures begin organically and often it is only once they become part of the mainstream that they are given a label. As John Lydon once said of punk: 'If you call it punk then it probably isn't.'

Subcultures often have 'purists' who chase the most authentic sounds, such as original Detroit techno and obscure 1960s soul records. With the advent of MTV, style tribes were put on display and their look was transported around the world, from the new romantics to hip hop.

Simon Reynolds, in his book *Energy Flash*, describes subcultures, particularly those within the dance music scene, as 'vibe tribes', where vibe is about having secret, specialist knowledge. He wrote: 'You can see it in those knowing smiles and the electric glances that pass around when a certain drop happens in a track, or a particular sound or riff comes in that creates synergy with the drugs that everyone's on . . . it's not elitist so much as tribal.'

Subcultures can inspire, influence and blend into one another. Hippies were a continuation of the beat movement, combined with a Californian surfer lifestyle, while Jamaica's rudeboys and London mods inspired the original skinheads. There's also a running theme of 'the hipster' – a word that emerged from Harlem in the 1920s from 'hip' or 'hep', meaning non-conformist and one step ahead.

It could be argued that subcultures are much less easy to define nowadays. They flourished at a time when young people would have to scrimp and save to buy the latest records and fashions and would therefore be more likely to follow one scene closely. But with the wide availability of music to be downloaded, pirated, and played on Spotify, people can access a huge range of genres and sounds, without having a particular allegiance.

Mainstream fashion has integrated deviant and bohemian cultures so that counterculture has become the dominant culture. Glastonbury Festival, for example, was founded in 1970 to be the British Woodstock, as part of the free festival movement, and was later adopted by punks and ravers. But it is now much more of a commercial venture, open to and embraced by a wide section of society – girls emulating Kate Moss in Hunter wellington boots and tiny shorts, middle-class parents with their children, and the super-rich.

In 1969, writer Nik Cohn perhaps offered the ultimate definition of what pop culture is. He said it's 'about clothes and cars and dancing, it's about parents and high school and being tied and breaking loose, it is about getting sex and getting rich and getting old, it's about America, it's about cities and noise. Get right down to it, it's about Coca-Cola.'

So where do fashion subcultures go from here? There are always new tribes growing organically that capture a particular mood and moment in society. We just don't know about them yet.

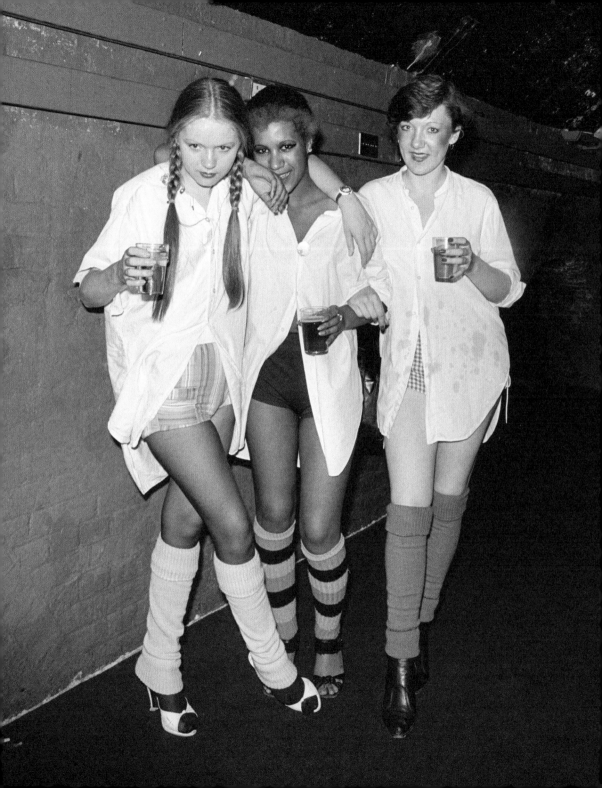

FLAPPER

In February 1920 *The Times* warned of the effects of the new 'frivolous scantily-clad, jazzing flapper, irresponsible and undisciplined, to whom a dance, a new hat or a man with a car is of more importance than the fate of nations.'

The twenties was a decade where women had unprecedented choices in how they lived their lives, with the flapper as the pleasure-seeking modern girl concerned only with parties, cocktails and shocking the older generation by bobbing her hair and revealing her body in exposing clothes. Prohibition in America created a secret nightlife where women could drink in illicit speakeasies or carry a hipflask of bootleg liquor.

The spirit of emancipation had been brewing since before the First World War, but it was the desperation of the war years, the shortage of men to marry, and new technology that changed the lives of young women more than earlier generations could have imagined. The gramophone, the cinema and the automobile brought a freedom to dating and leisure time, resulting in drunken car rides and petting or necking parties. The economy boomed but young people still bore the scars from the war, and they planned to live for every moment. A flapper recounted in *Outlook* magazine in 1922: 'We are the younger generation. The war tore away our spiritual foundations and challenged our faith. We are struggling to regain our equilibrium. The times have made us older and more experienced than you were at our age.'

The name 'flapper' has its roots in the seventeenth century, indicative of a fledgling bird flapping its wings for the first time. In the 1890s it was slang for a young prostitute, and just before the war it was used to mean a lively teenage girl. The word came into mainstream use around 1920 when Olive Thomas starred in the film *The Flapper*, and the lifestyle was depicted in Victor Margueritte's popular novel of 1922, *La Garçonne*, with a heroine who leaves her fiancé to dabble in lesbianism, drugs and single motherhood. The American actress Tallulah Bankhead was one of this new breed of women who shocked with saucy wisecracks: 'My father warned me about men and booze, but he never mentioned a word about women and cocaine.'

F. Scott Fitzgerald's wife, Zelda, was the model for the independent modern heroines who appeared in his short stories and novels like *The Beautiful and the Damned* and *The Great Gatsby*, a type he'd dubbed the 'mental baby vamp'. She wore rouge, held a cocktail as she laughed at rude jokes and drifted to sleep with her head on the shoulder of a man she'd just met. In 1922 Zelda described the original trailblazing flapper: 'She flirted because it was fun to flirt and wore a one-piece bathing suit because she had a good figure, she covered her face with powder and paint because she didn't need it and she refused to be bored chiefly because she wasn't boring.'

Bobbing the hair was one of the more shocking statements a woman could make, and while women had found short hair to be extremely comfortable during the war, it was still seen as a declaration of intent, as described in Fitzgerald's 1920 short story *Bernice Bobs Her Hair*. Bernice wishes to update her style to be more appealing to suitors and is asked if she believes in bobbed hair. 'I think it's unmoral,'

she replies gravely. 'But, of course, you've either got to amuse people or feed 'em or shock 'em.'

The fashion at the turn of the century was for women to have an 'S' shape, created through intricate and highly restrictive padding and corsetry. The war years introduced a practical chemise dress, loose fitting and belted at the waist, and after the war, women demanded more comfort, without the crushing of whalebone corsets and bustles.

By 1918 Coco Chanel was using the chemise style to create low-waisted dresses, and then simple geometric shift dresses in jersey and cotton which moved with the body. By 1925 it would become known as the *garçonne* look. Chanel would also popularise a trend for costume jewellery, with strings of faux pearls worn around the neck. The simple cloche hat, pulled over bobbed hair, would be the style of choice for the next decade.

Skirt lengths rose and fell in the first half of the 1920s according to what Paris fashions dictated, but in America they settled to above the knee by 1926. 'American flappers may be fickle but they know a good thing when they see it. And they intend to hang on to it,' said *The Flapper* magazine in 1922. Young women flattened down their chests and wore straight, sheer chemise dresses which created the illusion of nudity under shimmering and sequined fabrics, with arms and backs exposed. The female

Flappers drinking milkshakes, 1926

body was demystified, with women shaving their exposed armpits and showing off their legs, when twenty years before a glimpse of an ankle was considered scandalous. 'For the first time since civilisation began the world is learning that girls have knees,' the magazine noted.

Fashion incorporated Art Deco ethnic influences, with oriental designs and themes, Japanese prints and Egyptian hieroglyphics, inspired by the discovery of Tutankhamun's tomb in 1922. There was a fascination with African art, and fashionable women would wear wooden, African print or lacquered bracelets all the way up their arm. Nancy Cunard, an English heiress who moved to Paris's Left Bank, was known for her sharp bob, kohl eyes, and ivory and ebony bangles that would clink with every move.

The popularity of ragtime and jazz music from New Orleans grew, and dance moves like the black bottom, the shimmy and the foxtrot, which involved outrageously close contact, invaded the dance floors. While the charleston is now associated with *The Great Gatsby*, set in 1922, the dance didn't reach its peak until 1926. When jazz culture swept into Britain, it was seen by the older generation to be a threat to morals, particularly to young women who took to it with a fervent, sexual energy. Of course, not everyone was attending a Gatsby party – as *The Times* pointed out in 1920, most working-class women were still 'the domestic type' who wished to settle down. It was left largely to the middle or upper classes who could afford the decadence of the new style – the so-called Flaming Youth in the United States and Bright Young Things in Britain.

A 'freak' party in Chelsea, London, 1929

The capabilities of the body were tested with these fast and energetic jazz dances together with new sporting activities open to women like cycling and tennis. Jean Patou, known for his sportswear lines, created a daring sleeveless, knee-length tennis outfit for Suzanne Lenglen, the star of Wimbledon in 1921. She reflected the new athleticism of women and a desire for thinness. Exercise was changing the female body shape, and as the *Guardian* noted in 1928, 'the young flapper, even of fifteen, has not at the present day the "seventeen inch waist" her mother had; hockey, tennis, swimming, and calisthenics have broadened even the "little slip" at the waistline.'

With the explosion of film popularity – in the United States 35 million people were attending a screening on a weekly basis – movie stars became role models. Inspired by Colleen Moore in *Flaming Youth*, women cut their hair into short bob styles. Louise Brooks' glossy shingle cut was one of the most copied. Women's faces also became harder and more knowing, with black kohl eyes and defined lips, often shaped into a little, pouting cupid's bow. They wished to copy the beauty rituals of the stars they read about in *Photoplay* – when Bebe Daniels claimed she used oatmeal, buttermilk and honey on her skin, women across America took note. A survey in 1922 revealed that in the 18 to 30 age group, the most popular consumer items were hosiery, underwear, phonographs and records.

The Bright Young Things, a select group of upper-class thrillseekers, attracted publicity for their scavenger hunts, pranks and wild 'freak' parties, including a bath and bottle party, impersonation

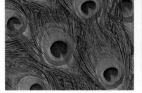

End of First
World War

Olive Thomas stars
in *The Flapper*

The Great Gatsby published

1918   1920 **FLAPPER** 1923   1925

Votes for women
in the United
Kingdom

The charleston

Skirts rise to
knee-length

1929
Wall Street crash

RIGHT Actress Dolores del Rio, 1929

parties and American parties where they dressed as 'hobos' and 'gold-diggers'. Characters like Elizabeth Ponsonby, Evelyn Waugh, Bryan Guinness and his fiancée Diana Mitford lived a life of endless luncheons and cocktail sessions, with Brenda Dean Paul recalling staying up until 5 or 6 a.m. every day for years. Their accents were clipped and they enjoyed wise-cracks and using exaggerations like 'marvellous', 'divine' and 'ghastly', to be heard over the noise of the gramophone or the chatter of cocktail parties. The Flaming Youth created their own lexicon to reflect their young, party-loving lifestyle: a manacle was an engagement ring, absent treatment was dancing with a shy partner, an alarm clock meant chaperone, and the bee's knees and cat's pyjamas was anything that was hot.

The 'old fogies' disapproved of the flapper's reckless behaviour, whether it was shingling their hair or drinking too much, rather than thinking of their future and settling down. Bright Young Thing Nancy Mitford constantly fought with her parents, as younger sister Jessica recalled: 'The hushed pall that hung over the house, meals eaten day after day in tearful silence, when Nancy at the age of twenty had her hair shingled . . . Nancy using lipstick, Nancy playing the newly-fashionable ukelele, Nancy wearing trousers, Nancy smoking a cigarette . . .'

The good times came to an abrupt end with the Wall Street Crash in 1929, followed by the Great Depression. Orders for couture and jewellery were cancelled in Paris and flappers were forced to cut back on the cocktails and dinner, lest they pay for it themselves.

Harlem, from around 1920 through to the end of Prohibition in 1933, was a self-contained black community where the sound of jazz filled the air, and where a renaissance in literature, fashion and arts, along with vibrant nightlife and a thriving gay scene, emerged and flourished.

Harlem, a New York City district of twenty-five blocks of late nineteenth-century brownstone townhouses and tenements, housed a growing black population following migration from the segregation of the south at the turn of the century. It was an enclosed world of black-owned businesses, entertainments and political and social life, and where black people paid for rent and services to each other. It was, as the *Independent* declared in 1921, the 'greatest negro city in the world, it boasts magnificent negro churches, luxurious negro apartment houses, vast negro wealth, and a negro population of 130,000, or possibly 150,000, or as enthusiasts declare, 195,000.'

Alain Locke's *The New Negro*, an anthology of fiction, poetry and essays, offered a collection of works by Harlem Renaissance writers like Claude McKay and Langston Hughes, who in May 1926 said in *The Nation*: 'We younger Negro artists who create now intend to express our individual dark-skinned selves without fear or shame. If white people are pleased we are glad. If they are not, it doesn't matter.'

At the turn of the century the black populations of northern cities were buying beauty products like hair oils and face creams, no matter their income, as it allowed a sense of control over their own image. A new dawn of self-confidence was evident, with fashion shows and beauty contests throughout Harlem and bountiful displays of black dolls in shop windows. The Savoy Ballroom held frequent pageants and balls on Saturday nights, which would be the most popular evening of the week. Despite this pride in colour, professional

PREVIOUS PAGE Harlem, New York c.1930 ABOVE Showgirls on stage in Harlem RIGHT Josephine Baker, 1925

dancers working in many parts of the United States were made to do the paper bag test – where their skin was not to be darker than the bag. Chorus girls would try to lighten their skin with lemon juice or cosmetics that offered promises of light mocha tones. Sarah Breedlove, known as Madam C.J. Walker, was the first female self-made millionaire in America and made her fortune with a line of beauty products for black women, including hair straighteners and growth stimulants. Her daughter A'Lelia Walker was known for her silver turban and for throwing the best 'queer' parties in Harlem. Wild rent parties, to help raise rent money with the sale of liquor in the kitchen, were held throughout Harlem on Saturday evenings while buffet flats were

after-hours private parties with drink and food, and where anything would go.

As jazz became the all-pervading musical genre, musicians like Louis Armstrong and Duke Ellington were celebrated and respected, and their pleasure in playing music brought them wealth and fame. But they still lived in a segregated world, and Harlem's entertainment proved to be an after-theatre draw for fashionable white Manhattan society who observed Harlem's people, as noted by Langston Hughes, 'like amusing animals, in a zoo.' Many of the thousands of white Americans who flocked to Harlem were jazz fans, while others wanted a taste of the exotic, as Harlem flouted liquor and homosexuality laws. White gay people would also journey to Harlem as

TOP LEFT Bessie Smith on stage BOTTOM LEFT Ma Rainey with 'Gabriel', Albert Wynn, Dave Nelson, Ed Pollack and Thomas Dorsey, c.1924–5

25

HARLEM RENAISSANCE   •

they could indulge at parties and nightclubs, and where either sex would expect to go home with a chorus girl or black musician. There were cabarets that described their dancers as 'tantalisin' tans' and 'hot chocolates', and these tourists would search out the 'real' experience of dancing the charleston or the black bottom at the Savoy or Cotton Club.

The Cotton Club, which opened in 1923, served up fried chicken and was decorated with African sculptures for primitive exoticism. Similarly the Plantation Club was done up like the antebellum South, with painted imagery of cotton plants and watermelons, a showboat and a 'mammy' cooking waffles in a log cabin for its white clientele who wanted a romanticised experience of the South.

While the most expensive nightclubs catered to white clientele, there were clubs with the real speakeasy atmosphere of cheap bootleg liquor and dances like the jitterbug. The *New York Times* reported in 1925 that in the Harlem clubs the most original steps were being performed only for black audiences. 'The negro dancers had come to realise that they would have to fight for their steps, and fight they would.'

After starting out as a chorus girl, Josephine Baker rose up the ranks to become the toast of Harlem nightspots, where 'she felt like a queen, roaring through the hot dusty nights in her ruffled taffeta frocks, fake pearl necklaces and big hats.' But in lower Manhattan she wasn't allowed in to Fifth Avenue stores or to choose where to sit in theatres.

Many black musicians who had fought in France during the war remained there as it was a more liberal alternative than America. Josephine Baker arrived in Paris to be presented as a Harlem jazz baby as well as an African fantasy figure in La Revue Negre. Her dance in a banana skirt, where she rolled her eyes, puffed her cheeks and left the stage on all fours, played up to this primitiveness. Such was Josephine Baker's celebrity in Paris that the designer Poiret created a pink fringed flapper gown especially for her, and she would wrap herself in the most luxurious costumes, fabrics and furs. After dancing with Baker in Paris, Hemingway raved she was 'the most sensational woman anybody ever saw . . . tall, coffee skin . . . legs of paradise, a smile to end all smiles . . . she was wearing a coat of black fur, her breasts handling the fur like it was silk.' As Langston Hughes said of the 1920s, 'it was the period when negroes were in vogue,' and this was particularly true in Europe.

After Florence Mills and her chorus girls the Blackbirds toured and performed in Mayfair, London, they became guests of honour and a source of fascination. British actress and socialite Brenda Dean Paul was particularly entranced: 'I feel so utterly at home with these enchanting people that every other white person in the room seemed positively genteel and almost indecently refined,' she said.

New social and sexual attitudes were particularly reflected in the music of the blues, and a thriving gay and lesbian community gathered at nightclubs

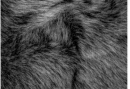

The lindy hop

| 1921 | 1925 | HARLEM RENAIS-SANCE | 1927 | 1933 |

1920
Prohibition
introduced

Broadway hit
Shuffle Along

Alain Locke's
The New Negro
published

Josephine Baker
arrives in Paris

Prohibition ends

RIGHT Seventh Avenue, Harlem, c.1927

including Lulu Belle's, in Harlem, a hangout for drag queens. Ma Rainey was known as the Mother of the Blues, and her 1928 song *Prove It On Me* includes the lyrics, 'Went out last night with a crowd of my friends. It must've been women, cause I don't like no men.' She was known for performing in top hat and tails, as was Gladys Bentley who drew in crowds at Harry Hansberry's Clam House on 133rd Street, with her heavy-set figure in a white tuxedo. They were typical of the 'bulldaggers', or female cross-dressers depicted in the Lucille Bogan song: 'BD women, you know they sure is rough, they drink up many a whiskey and they sure can strut their stuff.' Bessie Smith's first record in 1923, *Downhearted Blues*, sold 780,000 copies in six months. Originally from Tennessee, Ma Rainey took her under her wings when she joined the same revue and they toured the gin joints and brothels of the south. Bessie sang of lust and betrayal, putting her hurt out there for all to hear. She had huge appetites for soul food and liquor, never leaving a party until the booze was gone, as well as for affairs with chorus girls or piano players.

Harlem's famous drag balls of the 1920s allowed a safe space for cross-dressers to express themselves and would attract thousands of participants. It featured fashion parades where prizes were given to the best dressed and best looking. Singer and actress Ethel Waters would lend gay men her extravagant gowns, and remembered the 1920s as 'the great time of drags in Harlem with fashion parades for the male queers dressed in women's clothes.' The dresses could cost up to $500 and it was considered one of Harlem's most spectacular events. Ruby Smith, blues singer and niece of Bessie, noted that, 'some women wished they could look so good.'

This flare and expression of style in African American communities would be evident in following decades, as improvised fashion became an important show of pride and identity – from the zoot suit of the 1940s to the afro as a symbol of black power and the crisp 'b-boy' style in the 1970s.

'I wanna zoot suit with a reet pleat, with a drape shape and a stuff cuff, to look sharp enough to see my Sunday gal.' *A Zoot Suit*, L. Wolfe Gilbert and Bob O'Brien, 1942.

The zoot suit was a fashion crossover, from 1930s Harlem street style to Mexican Pachuco immigrant communities, from hepcat lindy hoppers to the cool white hipster just after the Second World War. The zoot suit came into public consciousness with the 1943 Zoot Suit riots in Los Angeles – the wearers were labelled as unpatriotic as they appeared to show indifference to the war by hanging out on the streets in flamboyant coloured or checked suits that breached fabric rationing and rebelled against societal norms.

The zoot's origins are thought to be around 1935, amongst jazz and swing musicians and the hipster crowd at Harlem's Savoy Ballroom, although there was a claim that the first zoot suit on record was early 1940 when a black bus worker in Georgia named Clyde Duncan ordered a copy of Rhett Butler's drape jacket from *Gone with the Wind*. The style was heavily influenced by jazz singer Cab Calloway, who wore a range of extravagant zoot suits on stage and in the 1943 film *Stormy Weather*.

The word 'hep' originated in the early days of jazz to refer to someone in the know, and as swing became more popular, the use of the word 'hip' became more widespread. Calloway published his own *Hepster Dictionary* in 1939, where he defined a hepcat as 'a guy who knows all the answers, understands jive'. 'Zoot' was hipster patter – a common term in the late 1930s within urban jazz culture, and also a Cajun word for 'cute', coming from the New Orleans jazz scene. The zoot suit was also referred to as a 'killer-diller coat' in Harlem slang.

The zoot look began to emerge in the working-class black, Hispanic and Filipino communities in the late 1930s as an audacious way to stand out. It meant an exaggerated and extravagant style, and the suits were all about making a dramatic impression – large padded shoulders, a long drape with wide lapels and high-waisted trousers that flared at the knee and tapered in at the ankle. It was worn with a wide-brimmed hat, ducktail hairstyle, two-tone pointed shoes and a long watch chain. The sometimes bright and bold colours and exaggerated structure was a refusal to be subservient, to stand out on the street in defiance and not to accept their designated place in the world. Some in the middle-class black community found the zoot suit an embarrassment, with its flagrant attention seeking and apparent disregard of the war effort.

In *Stylin': African American Expressive Culture*, it's noted that 'the zoot suit emerged at least as far back as the early 1930s . . . there was, however, a distinct shift somewhere around 1939 and 1940,' with suits becoming more exaggerated in size. In May 1943 the *Amsterdam News* playfully reported that the Duke of Windsor was the first zoot-suiter in the 1930s, and that on 'Seventh Avenue in New York, and on 47th Street in Chicago, the boys were wearing wide-brimmed hats, peg-top trousers and long coats.'

It became a popular style for lindy hoppers, first at the Savoy Ballroom in Harlem then across the country, as it was loose and allowed freedom of movement. Zoot suiters were the guys on the dancefloor who liked the very fast swing music which allowed them to show off both their clothes and their moves. Those who wore the zoot suit were young and disenfranchised, and their fashion choices gave them a sense of empowerment, particularly as it emulated black musicians like Dizzie Gillespie. It was a suit that bulked out their frame, making them more imposing, and the attitude had to be just as sharp. Thomas Sanchez wrote in his novel *Zoot-Suit Murders* in 1978: 'You got to be tricking yourself out like the dude, get yourself up in some pants with stuff-cuffs, reet-pleats, look like a zoot, walk like a zoot, talk like a zoot.'

The look was worn by Detroit Red, the young hustler who would become Malcolm X. In his autobiography he recalled the excitement of purchasing his first zoot suit at the age of fifteen, around 1940 – with bright blue trousers and a long coat that flared below the knees. His description emphasises the importance of striking the pose: 'I took three of those twenty-five cent sepia-toned, while-you-wait pictures of myself, posed the way 'hipsters' wearing their zoots would 'cool it' – hat angled, knees drawn close together, feet wide apart,

ABOVE College men in zoot suits, 1943 RIGHT Noe Vasquez and Joe Vasquez, after being attacked during the Zoot Suit Riots in Los Angeles, June 1943

both index fingers jabbed toward the floor. The long coat and swinging chain and the Punjab pants were much more dramatic if you stood that way.'

It was also adopted by young Mexican Americans, and became known as Pachuco style. They were the children of immigrants who had moved to the cities to seek work following a lack of rural jobs during the Great Depression. Urban neighbourhoods became barrios, and Pachuco gangs were formed as a reaction to feeling stuck between two worlds – experiencing racism and marginalisation, while losing a connection to their heritage. Their way of rebelling was through the zoot suit, with its origins

in the black community. A 1942 *Newsweek* story recorded the Pachucos in vivid, garish suits, with polka-dot shirts, 'string ties, pearl buttons as big as silver dollars, and trousers so tight they have to be zipped.' 'We were a minority group of a minority group,' wrote activist Cesar Chavez, 'So, in a way, we were challenging cops by being with two or three friends and dressing sharp. But in those days, I was prepared for any sacrifice to be able to dress the way I wanted to dress. I thought it looked sharp and neat, and it was the style.'

An extravagant amount of fabric was required for a zoot suit, contravening fabric rationing that

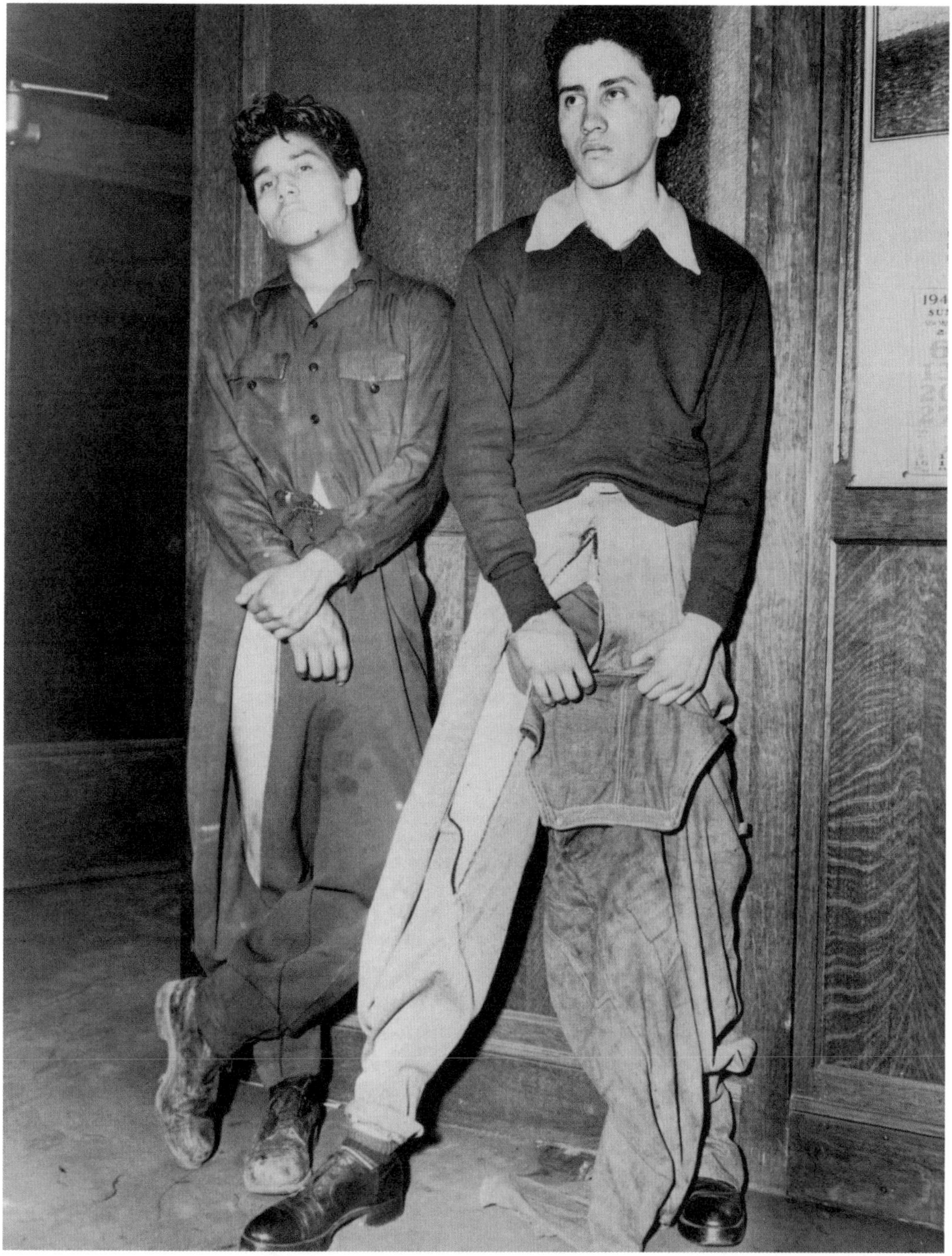

Zoot Suit Riots

1940   THE ZOOT SUIT   1942   1943

1938
Jitterbug goes mainstream

Fabric rationing in
the United States

Cab Calloway stars
in *Stormy Weather*

was introduced in 1942. Cab Calloway's *Stormy Weather* suit, said to cost $185, was made before rationed orders were put in place. 'Jitterbug dancers and the strange, voluminous garb that many of them affect are interfering with the progress of the country's war effort and the War Production Board intends to do something about it,' wrote the *New York Times* in 1942. 'It is wasting a large amount of fabric that ought to be saved for our soldiers and for necessary civilian clothing.' The self-assertiveness and audacity of zoot-suiters, combined with a disregard for rationing at a time of war, exasperated the American majority.

With limited places for youths to go, they were more likely to cause trouble in the streets. In autumn 1942 *Life* magazine said: 'Suddenly the country is aware of what war is doing to children. American youth is on the same kind of lawless rampage that swept England during 1940.' The world war brought simmering racial tensions to the surface as young GIs blew off steam before being shipped out to danger zones, drinking in late-night bars and roaming streets in their down time. This clash of culture culminated in the June 1943 Zoot Suit riots in Los Angeles where stationed servicemen entered black and Hispanic neighbourhoods, dragging zoot-suiters from streetcars, cinemas and buses, ripping off and burning their clothes, and cutting their longer hair. The press and police were more sympathetic to the servicemen than the zoot-suiters, who were stripped, beaten and humiliated. The local authorities banned the zoot suit and closed down areas to servicemen, but riots spread to other cities including Philadelphia, Detroit and Montreal.

ABOVE Guardarrama Tapia and Jesus Gonzalez de la Rosa in Pachuco outfits, Mexico City, 2014

After the war ended and rationing was relaxed, the zoot suit became more mainstream. By 1948 a slimmer version was marketed to white men as a 'bold look', and worn by white jazz aficionados like Bing Crosby who would take on elements of what was originally a black fashion. They were what Norman Mailer referred to as 'the white negro', listening to Charlie Parker and smoking weed, or 'tea'. Artie Shaw described Crosby as 'the first hip white person born in the United States'.

The Pachuco style is still active in Mexico City, referencing the audacious style of dress of the 1940s Los Angeles Latino communities and where Pachucos dress in vibrant and colourful handmade zoot suits. As the *Guardian* reported in 2014, 'many modern Pachucos in Mexico follow on from this custom and use the suits not only to go dancing, but also as a continuing sign of protest against the treatment of Mexican immigrants north of the border.'

SWING KID

Swingjugend, or swing youth, were teenage swing fans in Nazi Germany who rejected the Hitler Youth in favour of jazz. They chose British and American dress, deregulation longer hair and a carefree way of life that deviated from Hitler's uniform brownshirts and his ideal of a blonde mass of tanned, strong and obedient people.

The Third Reich was threatened by the expressive, individual nature of jazz – the opposite of the strict uniformity of the Nazis. For many teenagers, Hitler Youth offered a new sense of pride and purpose but swingjugend chose a different attitude. As Hamburg swing kid Tommie Scheel once said, 'We wanted to tell all these dumb bastards that we were different, that was all.' Matt Wolf, whose documentary *Teenage* covers youth groups before the end of the war, described Tommie Scheel as 'the hippest of them all, smuggling swing records and British fashion into Germany to rebel against the Nazi regime. He is almost like a proto-Punk, you could say.'

Swing music was hot jazz with a big band accompaniment, speeding up the tempo to create the frenzied sounds of 'Let's Dance' and 'Sing, Sing, Sing'. Benny Goodman and his orchestra reached furious popularity in America by 1937, attracting a mass crowd of adoring fans who would go wild. As Goodman would say, 'they were the show and we were the audience.'

American male swings wore a style influenced by black urban dress, with baggy trousers, long jackets, long chains from belt to pocket, and pork-pie hats. Female swing fans wore a more informal style of blouses, sweaters, flat shoes, short white bobby socks and a short pleated dress to swing when dancing. Benny Goodman orchestra vocalist Helen Ward said: 'when the lindy really caught on, the gals began wearing saddle shoes.'

Swing orchestras were likely to be mixed race, and jitterbug and lindy hop dances came straight out of Harlem, so it was inevitable that the Nazis would detest it. German eugenicists argued that black people had no sexual control, as evident in jazz, a beat they said would corrupt Nordic women. If jazz was *entartete musik*, or degenerate music, then swing, with Jewish composers and black musicians, was much worse.

While the Weimer Republic of the 1920s saw hot American jazz as the essence of modernism, having encouraged a rich nightlife of theatre, large orchestras in plush hotels and a deviant cabaret scene, the Nazi party would try to stamp it out. Under the Third Reich musicians required a membership card to play and black and Jewish musicians faced harassment at Berlin nightspots. In 1938, American newspapers reported that Nazi leaders 'declared today that swing music may be fit for Negroes and Jews, but not for us Germans.'

Despite this, jazz continued to be played in cities across Germany and a small, elite group of jazz purists kept it alive at hot clubs, where they circulated records, and by listening to Radio Luxemberg and BBC London. 'Swing is the thing in Germany,' reported the New York Times in 1937. 'At least in Hamburg and Berlin, where there are modernistic night clubs and imported jazz bands, the fashionable young German women and men do their dancing to swing music. With the rhythm of Harlem hoofers they keep time to the band, and en masse they look like many puppets, each jerked by a separate set of wires.'

In 1936 a swing club was founded in Dusseldorf where members adopted English names and greeted each other with 'Swing High!' In Frankfurt, the Harlem Club regulars also wore an English style of dress, and acknowledged each other in the street by whistling a secret section of swing music. But it was in Hamburg that the scene was really swinging. They were wealthier than their Berlin counterparts and could afford to indulge in the finer things. While American swing fans dressed in baggy suits and a more relaxed style for girls, in Germany their dress was inspired by the Hollywood movies that Joseph Goebbels, Reich Minister of Propaganda, would allow to be screened.

Female swings looked to the glamour of Hollywood with long, shiny hair instead of the traditional German braid. They pronounced their femininity with painted nails and lips, shorter skirts, blouses and silk stockings. The boys wore custom-tailored suits, sometimes with a Glen check, crepe-soled shoes, white silk scarves and trenchcoats swung over the top. To add British flair, they sported felt or homburg hats, a Union Jack badge on their lapel, and they carried umbrellas or perhaps a copy of The Times under their arm. Their dress, as Michael Kater wrote in Different Drummers, 'had to be shown off in public, and so the swings developed the habit of leisurely sauntering up and down Hamburg's most fashionable streets . . . during rush hour.' Jazz pianist Jutta Hipp joined the Hot Club Leipzig. During air raids she would sneak downstairs to listen to foreign radio, noting down the melodies. She said: 'I used to wear blue silk stockings with a red seam, red hearts on the knee, and as teenagers do, wanting to be different, would walk a whole block backwards to see if anyone gets upset and then smile at them.'

They bought and traded records for private parties or would attend mass swing dances at Café Heinze or Trocadero. Instead of swing and jazz, the Nazis would try to encourage the uptake of outmoded dances like the waltz but this seemed to have a limited effect on the swingheinis. Swings were generally apolitical, defining themselves as lottern, or lazy and carefree, but the pressure to join the Hitler Youth increased in

Kaffeehaus Lausen
Reeperbahn 56/60

So

bleibt Dir Kritik erspart

Nicht erlaubt

ist diese Art!

Benny Goodman is
the star of swing

1938

SWING KID

1939

1935

Nazi Party bans
foreign radio

Jewish musicians banned
from playing in Germany

1942
Swing kids sent to
concentration camps

RIGHT Zazou, Paris, c.1943

the lead up to the war. While the Gestapo could arrest them and forcibly cut their hair, the Nazis didn't have a set way to deal with these problems. The prohibitions on public parties led to a rise in gatherings within the safe confines of their parents' villas, where they could serve wine and cognac and play swing on the gramophone. Toast of the party scene were the charming Inga and Jutta Madlung, daughters of a half-Jewish lawyer. They would do a pitch perfect imitation of American harmony singers the Andrews Sisters and had a reputation for engaging freely in casual sex.

The clampdown on jazz was loosened at various times during the war. During permissive stages the swing kids would throw all caution to the wind. Not only did they ignore curfews, they would listen to the BBC and play jazz in public shelters. Tommy Scheel and friends would disrupt the newsreels in cinemas and make sarcastic comments in front of the Gestapo, leading to them being arrested and interrogated in October 1940. As the war went on, punishment became more severe as record collectors found to be in possession of Jewish jazz could face labour camps, and Scheel was taken to a concentration camp to carry out hard labour. It's estimated that 40 to 70 swings were sent to camps from 1942 to 1944, with

parents of swings also being sent away, particularly if they had Jewish heritage.

Inga and Jutta Madlung arrived at Ravensbrück concentration camp in summer 1942, where they suffered sadistic cruelty. Inga was almost blinded after being made to look at the sun for days, and was forcibly injected with a weight-gaining product to supposedly suppress her libido. At the Bergen-Belsen trials, Jutta Madlung told the court they were sent there 'because of political jokes which I made, because I had a Jewish female friend, and because I had English gramophone records.'

A similar rebellious swing scene in wartime France sprung up in the Latin quarter of Paris. Known as 'zazou', they held secret parties, dressed in striped suits with bright coloured socks, oiled their hair, sported Clark Gable moustaches and smoked English cigarettes despite the rationing in place. Female zazou dressed in roll neck sweaters, bum freezer jackets, pleated skirts and big, flat shoes. Their hair was worn in a bun and they painted lips and nails red. Punishments handed out included having their heads forcibly shaved. After a forced labour draft in 1942, the zazou disappeared underground, many paring down their dress to enter the French Resistance.

BEATNIK

The beat generation was a group of young, postwar idealists who rejected consumerism and looked to a type of spiritualism as expressed through writing and being. It began in New York at the end of the Second World War, flourished in San Francisco and Venice Beach and then spread out to Paris, Mexico City and Tangier with enclaves of beats in dark clothing, smoking weed and carrying their notebooks filled with drawings and poetry.

The beat movement encompassed a bohemian, revolutionary existence involving hitchhiking, jazz, eastern philosophy and left-wing politics. Jack Kerouac spoke of his vision in the late 1940s, 'of a generation of crazy, illuminated hipsters suddenly rising and roaming America, serious, bumming and hitchhiking everywhere, ragged, beatific, beautiful in an ugly graceful new way.' It was a second lost generation of men demobilised from the army, and now drifting across America in their jeans and t-shirts, like Montgomery Clift on screen in 1950, hitching at the side of the road.

They revelled in their own poverty, and the style of dressing was said to come from having no money. French beatnik icon Juliette Greco described being a teenager in Paris with only 'one dress and one pair of shoes, so the boys in the house started dressing me in their old black coats and trousers. A fashion was shaped out of misery.'

'As our hair grew longer, we were inventing a style,' beat poet Michael McClure said. 'I was poor – everyone was poor. I'd climb into my old station wagon, the door tied shut with a piece of rope, and drive for forty minutes from San Francisco to the top of Mount Tamalpais.' They embraced world travel and respected nature, living the philosophy of Kerouac's generation-defining novel *On the Road*. 'The first hipsters were a far cry from the affected zombielike "cool" stance that came to predominate later,' said journalist Lester Bangs in *Rolling Stone*.

Kerouac first introduced the term 'beat' in 1948, defining an anti-conformist, beaten-down movement in New York. Together with Allen Ginsberg,

PREVIOUS PAGE 'We Hitch-hiked to the Sun', *Picture Post*, 1954 RIGHT, CLOCKWISE FROM TOP LEFT Jack Kerouac, New York, 1959; French actress and singer Juliette Greco, 1965; the Gaslight coffee house in Greenwich Village, New York, 1959

William Burroughs and Neal Cassady, the inspiration for the character Dean Moriarty, he formed a close-knit group of writers and poets, inspired by the black and Puerto Rican communities in Harlem. They were Norman Mailer's 'white negro' – jazz lovers who talked hip and smoked 'tea'. They would spend days and nights at Greenwich Village loft parties or twenty-four-hour cafes, talking and creating, looking at downward rather than upward mobility, to form ideas on life and literature.

They romanticised the lowlife groups of prostitutes, junkies and drunks who dwelled around Times Square and its seedy cinemas, all-night cafeterias and peep shows. Kerouac and Ginsberg's 'spontaneous bop prosody' writing style was like the expressionist freestyle jazz of Charlie Parker and Miles Davis, Jackson Pollock's art and Marlon Brando's method acting. James Dean was photographed wandering empty Manhattan streets in a huge, bulky coat; he played the bongo, and his jeans and t-shirts spoke to a generation as the uniform of a rebel.

Respectable women were expected to be chaste, but beat women lived in East Village dives by themselves or with men they weren't married to, they rolled their own cigarettes, or set off cross-country on a Greyhound bus. Writer Joyce Johnson, who had a relationship with Kerouac, wrote: 'Yes indeed we suffered. We were poor, sometimes even hungry; we had holes in our black stockings and wore thriftshop clothes . . . at times we were frightened. We had orphaned ourselves by becoming "bad women" so we had no one to fall back on. We took terrible chances with our bodies when we had illegal abortions,' but, 'we experienced the thrill of being part of a movement that changed life in America, and we endured the hard times in making something new.'

When Kerouac's *On The Road* was published in 1957, it sparked a fascination with this alternative way of living, encouraging women to be unconventional and experimental. Ann Douglas, a nineteen-year-old from New Jersey, remembered that in June 1959, 'just after I was expelled from high school, I dyed my hair black, caught a New York-bound train and checked into a YWCA near Times Square under an assumed name.' That is, until her stepfather hired a detective to come and find her. Beat girls rejected the 1950s beauty salon aesthetic in favour of black leotards and long straight hair, a look that was mysterious and cool. Sonic Youth's Kim Gordon recalled: 'When I was little, my dad and I went to visit one of those Venice beatnik guys, though I mostly remember his glam girlfriend with her long, straight black hair, her red-polished fingernails, and her guitar. She was the first beatnik I ever met. I sat in her lap, thinking, I wish my mom were as cool as this.'

By 1954 the New York crowd had regrouped in San Francisco, where a poetry movement grew around the City Lights bookstore in the Italian-American enclave of North Beach. Ginsberg debuted his poem *Howl* at City Lights in October 1955. It was a shocking depiction of a gay man associating with junkies, prostitutes and black musicians. Like Burroughs's novel *Naked Lunch*, about the horrors of addiction, it would come under fire from the restrictive obscenity laws of the time.

North Beach attracted those who were first named 'beatniks' by the *San Francisco Chronicle* in 1958, and tourists flocked to the coffee houses and bookstores to watch them play bongo drums while

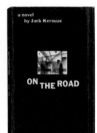

Beats arrive in
San Francisco

1953

On The Road published

Audrey Hepburn
in Funny Face

Term 'beatnik' coined

1957   **1958**

BEATNIK

1948
Jack Kerouac in
New York

HOWL
AND OTHER POEMS
ALLEN GINSBERG
Introduction by
William Carlos Williams

ON THE ROAD

sitting in hazy marijuana-filled basement bars. They were given the stereotypical image of a goatee, a beret, black polo necks and moccasins.

Venice Beach, a run-down former pleasure beach, was home to a number of communes and beat coffee houses, not necessarily for naïve teenagers – they could be Harvard graduates who rejected a life of working in advertising, or a wife who ran away from home when she realised she needed more from life. In Venice Beach, beat men went barefoot or wore sandals, and, according to Lawrence Lipton's study, they grew beards as a way to 'reject the rewards of the goddam dog-eat-dog society.'

Beatniks became a character staple in movies, representing the sinister in films like *The Beat Generation* (1959) and *The Beatniks* (1960), and the stylish, when Audrey Hepburn visits subterranean Parisian dives in *Funny Face* (1956). 'In the 1950s America has been besieged from within by bearded men in green berets and sandals and by women in Levi's made up like German silent-film actresses, a self-styled beat generation speaking in a jam session slang and caught up in a tarantism of jazz,' wrote the *New York Times* in 1959. Resentment grew amongst

the serious poets and artists as journalists blamed the beatniks for every crime and incident in America. By 1958 the fashions of beatniks eclipsed the writings of the beats. Kerouac, in his red lumberjack shirt, couldn't recognise this new incarnation. He said to Ginsberg: 'I discovered a new beat generation a long time ago, I hitchhiked and starved, for art, and that makes me the fool of the beatniks with a crown of shit. Thanks, America.'

In New York, journalists and ad men began sprouting beards and wearing elkskin shoes, 'the lap-over Indian moccasin kind that no beatnik could ever afford to buy.' By 1960, beatnik fashion had crossed into high-end designs. 'It was clear that the beatnik-heiress look is the latest to roll off the Seventh Avenue cutting boards,' wrote the *New York Times*. Girls would wear their beat look at the weekends, when they could get away with carefree, casual dressing and off-the-shoulder tops. It was a 'gilded bohemia', but without the poverty and suffering. The cool beat girl would become sexualised, with a Miss Beatnik competition in 1959 at Venice Beach and *Playboy* magazine introducing actress and model Yvette Vickers as a 'Beat Playmate'.

Greenwich Village beatniks, New York, 1959

In the 1960s, some beats would morph into hippies, while enclaves would continue in London and Paris, with students in duffel coats, long hair and black sunglasses. In London trad jazz fans emulated the beats and Paris existentialists with jumpers, duffel coats, scarves and paint-splattered jeans. The actress Jean Seberg, with her cropped hair and striped top, and Brigitte Bardot, in polo necks and jeans, would continue a chic beat style.

Kerouac's movement would have a continuous hold on culture. In 1993 Gap advertised with the slogan 'Kerouac wore khakis', and William Burroughs would reflect 'on the awesome power of the word. Kerouac's *On the Road* sold millions of Levi's and created thousands of espresso bars to serve their wearers. His book launched a children's crusade to Paris, Tangier, Kathmandu, Goa, Mexico, Columbia, winning converts everywhere.'

TEDDY BOY

With the look of a western gunfighter and a name that referred to a period in Britain's regal history, the Teddy boys were the rebellious British postwar youth movement who drummed to the back-beat of rock'n'roll and grabbed attention by the way they dressed. They fused the historic with the current, combining two opposing worlds – the dandified upper-class Edwardians and the new egalitarian style coming from America.

But with their confident, proud style came perceived menace. Ten years before the infamous seaside battles between the mods and rockers, young Teds were also reported to be tearing up seaside resorts on bank holiday weekends. They wore a gang uniform that demanded respect, they accessorised with sharpened combs, chains and studded belts for fighting, and their apparent vicious delinquency played out in the media. In 1953 the *Daily Mirror* headlined with 'Flick Knives, Dance Music and Edwardian Suits', following a Clapham Common gang fight in which a seventeen-year-old, John Beckley, was murdered by youths wearing Edwardian-style suits. At the trial, a group of girls wearing drape jackets with pencil skirts came to show their support and referred to those on trial as 'Teddy boys', with Teddy as a shortened version of Edward, and the name stuck.

Parts of society in the 1950s felt afraid of a tough, independently-minded working-class youth who had been raised during a time of war, had experienced rationing and would go into national service at eighteen years old. But many of the Teds were simply dressing up, and when Britain was swept up with rock'n'roll in 1955, the Ted became one of the most popular youth looks. Johnny Rotten, whose punk image would be inspired by the Teds, remembered: 'I must have been only four but I was very impressed looking at the Teddy boys on the street corner. Their audacious colours and sheer toughness. They demanded you pay attention to them.'

PREVIOUS PAGE A yound Teddy boy in Tottenham, London, 1954 ABOVE Sheffield Teddy boys

The Second World War put an end to an expression of style that had flourished in the 1920s and 1930s with boaters and Oxford shoes, a dandified look that didn't suit the hardships of war. Thousands of American servicemen who were based in Britain for the war brought with them American fashions and swing music, flooding the dancehalls with the jive and lindy hop. The dominant American look of the time was baggy jackets and trousers, and hair worn like Hollywood star Tony Curtis – short, greased and with a quiff.

Britain in the early 1950s was still emerging from the postwar gloom with austerity and continued rationing, and cities with rubble where buildings used to be. As a reaction against America as the new world leader, Savile Row tailors like Hardy Amies produced an outfit for the upper classes which nostalgically referenced the reign of Edward VII, a time of confidence, wealth and a definitive class system. Trousers were narrowed to sixteen inches, worn with a long jacket and small bowler hat. They were named the New Mayfair Edwardians and were photographed by Norman Parkinson for British Vogue in April 1950, standing proudly in their suits, harking back to the smart style of the Edwardians. This look filtered into London's Soho as it proved popular with gay men, and was swiftly picked up by national media.

By 1952 groups of working-class teenagers were inspired by news articles to appropriate the Savile Row New Edwardians, turning something that had been designed for the wealthy and connected into a statement against the class system. Kids across the country took to wearing drape jackets with small lapels and trousers sixteen inches or

ABOVE Teddy boys queueing to have their hair styled in Hounslow, London, 1953 FOLLOWING PAGES Teddy girls pose in the East End of London, 1955; Teddy boy, 1955

narrower. They couldn't afford the Savile Row suits, but they would devote any expendable income on perfecting the look, which was quite separate from mainstream fashion. Suits were embellished with an Edwardian-style watch chain, a brocade or Paisley waistcoat and a cheesecutter cap. Trousers had a 'guardsman's fall' to show their coloured or Pringle-pattern socks. They added flourishes of the new American rebels they saw on screen. Hair was greased into different shapes, including the mohawk and duck's arse. Some Teds, if they were old enough to grow them, accessorised with Elvis-inspired short sideburns. Brylcreem dispensers were available at the municipal baths, so Teddy boys could always maintain their sculpted hair.

Like Western movie heroes, drape jackets were worn long and swaggering, with a roll collar or touches of extravagant velvet. Towards the end of the fifties, inspired by Chuck Berry and the characters in TV series *Maverick*, gambler's boot string ties would be held together with unusual, decorative medallions including insects and skulls.

As well as the Chelsea boot, the Ted shoe of choice was the brothel creeper. It originated in the Second World War, when British soldiers bought chukka boots or desert boots from the markets of Egypt and Burma. They had a tough crepe sole to keep feet warm at night and cool during the day. Soldiers liked them so much they wore them in seedy nightclubs back home, where they earned the name brothel creeper for their quietness. Adapted and sold by George Cox in 1949, they were given more pronounced soles. In later Ted revivals, the brothel creeper was elevated by a couple of inches.

The new Mayfair
Edwardians

Blackboard Jungle
released

Clapham Common murder trial

1950

TEDDY BOY

1953

1955

1949

George Cox creates the
brothel creeper

The original Teds were pre-rock'n'roll, instead dancing to jive or blues musicians like Hank Williams and Sugar Chile Robinson on the jukeboxes that would transport them to utopian America. But as soon as rock'n'roll arrived in 1954 with Bill Haley's 'Shake, Rattle and Roll', they were hooked – it represented their energy, youth and rebelliousness.

The media was unsure what to make of rock'n'roll and the young fans it garnered, particularly with increased black immigration to the country. The *Daily Mail* advised its readers: 'It is deplorable. It is tribal. And it is from America . . . Rock and roll is sexy music. It can make the blood race. It has something of the African tom-tom and voodoo dance.'

Teds celebrated the release of the 1955 film *Blackboard Jungle* by rioting at cinemas across Britain. Bill Haley's 'Rock Around the Clock' had a similar effect as Teds took over cinemas by dancing in the aisles and cutting up the seats with their razor knives. Cinemas resorted to signs saying 'No Edwardian Clothing'. This violence would grab headlines, and following the 1958 Notting Hill riots, with groups of Teddy boys carrying out assaults on the Caribbean community, lead to the movement's eventual decline by the early 1960s.

It was boredom that encouraged the delinquency of the Teds, according to writer Stanley Cohen. They 'were reacting not so much against "adults" but the little that was offered in the fifties: the cafe, the desolate town, the pop culture of the dance halls, Locarnos and Meccas aimed at the over-twenties. Their style was adopted from a different social group – the Edwardian dandy – and its exaggeration and ritualisation were mirrored in the groups' activities:

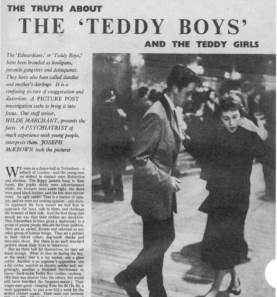

ABOVE LEFT 'The Truth About The Teddy Boys', *Picture Post*, 1954   ABOVE RIGHT Teddy boy revival, London, 1972

a certain brutality, callousness, indifference and almost stoicism.' In 1956 the *Daily Mirror* quoted Mark, a nineteen-year-old labourer: 'I think the older generation have got the needle. They're always saying they worked for the younger generation to have better times than they had in their young days. Well, we've got that better time and they've got the needle because we are happy.'

Ted girls were often overlooked, but as well as the girls in pencil skirts, conical bras and beehives, and fuller, petticoated skirts as the fifties progressed, there were groups who dressed in Ted style. They wore black or oatmeal drape jackets, with shin-length pencil skirts, pedal pushers with roll ups, slip-on shoes and sometimes carried an umbrella for the gentlemanly look. Film director Ken Russell took

rare photos of Teddy girls, standing proud amongst a derelict, bombed-out building. One of the girls, fifteen-year-old Rose Shine, recalled to the *Sunday Times*: 'We were all right. We got slung out of the picture house for jiving up the aisles once, but we never broke the law. We weren't drinkers. We'd go to milk bars, have a peach melba and nod to the music, but you weren't allowed to dance. It was just showing off: "Look at us!"'

In the 1970s a huge rock'n'roll revival saw new Teddy boys, nicknamed 'plastics' by the originals of the early 1950s, sporting more pronounced brothel creepers, velvet drapes and larger quiffs. The look and attitude of the Ted would also be evident in the punk movement, as a voice of dissent amid the hardships of the times.

GREASER & ROCKER

When Marlon Brando terrorised the residents of a small town in *The Wild One* in 1953, the film was considered so dangerous that it was banned in Britain. But it would inspire a generation of rockers in the United Kingdom, and greasers in the United States, where the uniform was jeans and black leather and the soundtrack was rock'n'roll.

Ever since *American Graffiti* and *Happy Days* in the 1970s, rock'n'roll has been considered synonymous with the birth of the American teenager – the baby boomers born at the end of the Second World War who were a new consumerist force with a disposable income from working or from their affluent parents. They used their cash to express their own style through music and fashion. Rock'n'roll fans rebelled against square mainstream 1950s culture, and took an anti-authoritarian stance. Their heroes were musicians like Gene Vincent, Eddie Cochran and Elvis Presley who shook up rockabilly. Coming from below the Mason-Dixon line, it combined a blues rhythm with a snare drum, the African American sounds of jazz, gospel and blues with hillbilly country and western, bringing together a dangerously mixed audience.

Fats Domino's 'The Fat Man' of 1949 is considered the first rock'n'roll record, Chuck Berry was the first to incorporate an electric guitar and in 1954 Elvis recorded 'That's All Right' at Sun Records in Memphis. But it was Bill Haley's huge hit 'Rock Around the Clock', featured in *Blackboard Jungle* in 1955, which set rock'n'roll in motion. The film depicted wild, disinterested teenagers who in one scene, destroy the jazz records of their teacher. Rock'n'roll spoke to teenagers about high school, teen love, and having to do the chores. But it was also dangerously sexual – the lyrics could be slyly crude, and Elvis's hip thrusts were like a mating ritual.

OPENING PAGE Rockers in the Ace Cafe, London, 1964 PREVIOUS PAGE Teenage hot rod enthusiasts, Scrivners Drive-In coffee shop, Los Angeles, 1950 ABOVE Rocker leathers RIGHT Gene Vincent, Hollywood, 1956

Jukeboxes, *American Bandstand* and record shops meant that the rock'n'roll sound circulated in cafes and amongst groups of teenagers. Rock'n'roll girls wore wide circular skirts, known as poodles, which flared up as they danced. They had tight sweaters, bobby socks and a scarf knotted around their necks; their hair was often pulled into a high ponytail or worn in the style of actress Natalie Wood.

Greasers can be linked to the same beginnings as the beats. They were both postwar countercultures founded by rebels who looked to the music of African Americans, and were represented by James Dean and Jack Kerouac as new rebellious archetypes in jeans and t-shirts. Greasers were the working-class, motorhead version of the beat, and by the 1960s they offered a grounding of masculinity amongst the poets and intellectuals of New York and San Francisco.

The name 'greaser' came from their greased-up hair and was originally a derogatory reference to Mexicans. Greasers liked nothing more than rockabilly and hot rod cars, they were often thought of as juvenile delinquents with an ethnic Latino or Italian-American background and from broken homes. Gangs offered a sense of belonging, and their leathers had the name of their gang emblazoned on the back – they could be draped over the shoulders of a girl they were going steady with, as another symbol of possession.

In S.E. Hinton's *The Outsiders*, set in the mid-1960s, the greasers were gangs of poor rock'n'roll lovers who thought Elvis was 'tuff' and the Beatles were 'rank'. As described by Ponyboy Curtis in the novel, 'We wear our hair long and dress in blue jeans and t-shirts, or leave our shirttails out and wear leather jackets and tennis shoes or boots.' The hair

was vitally important. 'Our hair labelled us greasers, too – it was our trademark. The one thing we were proud of. Maybe we couldn't have Corvairs and madras suits, but we could have hair.'

The classic rocker look of white t-shirt, jeans and leather jacket evolved from the late 1940s US motorcycle gangs, who were hard-drinking, hard-fighting ex-GIs who struggled to adapt to home life. Some morphed into Hell's Angels and outlaw motorcycle gangs, wearing their leather jackets from the airforce, with turn-up jeans, boots and a motorcycle cap, and a t-shirt that could be stripped into rags to mop up grease. Jeans, adopted by motorbike gangs for their toughness and durability, had originally been designed in the nineteenth century as practical workwear for labourers and miners, and would later be seen as a romanticised cowboy uniform, worn on farms and in the great outdoors of the Midwest.

In 1947 an invasion of motorcycle gangs in a California town called Hollister made exaggerated national headlines and was the focus of a *Life* magazine photo spread. The town had been the host of an annual motorcycle race, but it wasn't prepared for around four thousand motorcyclists to descend, as they drank, fought, vandalised buildings and performed stunts. This story would become the basis for *The Wild One*, depicting the Black Rebel Motorcycle Gang, who wore jackets emblazoned with the name, leather bike caps, gloves and jeans with turn ups. 'What are you rebelling against Johnny?'

a girl asks Marlon Brando in the film. 'What you got?' he sneers. It was this that was terrifying to the older generation – anti-social behaviour just for the hell of it, and jeans allowed teenagers to buy into that attitude. Marlon Brando recounted in his autobiography: 'I had fun making it, but never expected it to have the impact it did. I was as surprised as anyone when t-shirts, jeans and leather jackets suddenly became symbols of rebellion . . . sales of leather jackets soared.'

Greaser style diverged from typical male fashion – away from the suits and hats, for the look of the blue-collar worker. 'The greaser's life was a physicalised one, in keeping with conceptions of working-class life as being centred on manual labour, industrial machinery and simple pleasures. The greaser may have listened to black rock and roll, but did not emulate black social attitudes or behaviour,' wrote Daniel Marcus in *Happy Days and Wonder Years*.

In many ways, 1959 was the death of rock'n'roll in America. It was marked by the plane crash that killed Buddy Holly, The Big Bopper and Ritchie Valens, Elvis joining the army, and Jerry Lee Lewis marrying his thirteen-year-old cousin. In 1960 Eddie Cochran was killed in a car crash, while touring in the UK, a country in the grips of rock'n'roll fever, fascinated with the glamour of American stars. Marty Wilde met Eddie Cochran when he arrived in Britain: 'The first thing I noticed about Eddie was his complexion. We British lads had acne, and

1953
Marlon Brando in
The Wild One

Elvis Presley at
Sun Records

1955

GREASER
& ROCKER

Bill Haley's 'Rock Around The Clock'

1959

Buddy Holly killed
in plane crash

1964

Rockers and
mods clash

TOP LEFT Rockers outside the Ace Cafe, London, 1964 BOTTOM LEFT Teenagers crowd around the Paramount Theatre in New York to see *Don't Knock the Rock*, 1957

Eddie walked in with the most beautiful hair and the most beautiful skin – his skin was a light brown, a beautiful colour with all that California sunshine, and I thought, "you lucky devil".'

As the Teddy boy was becoming passé, the rocker emerged as a reaction to mod fashions. Stanley Cohen, in *Folk Devils and Moral Panics*, believed the rockers saw 'the Teddy boys becoming too respectable – a few years before the end of the decade, Teddy boy suits were already being sold at jumble sales – and they went directly to the old American "Wild Ones" theme: the black leather, the motor-bikes, the metal studs.'

Motorbikes were a cheap mode of transport for the rockers, also known as ton-up boys or the coffee bar cowboys. Their lifestyle centred around the British cafe culture, where they could race ton-up, at speeds of more than 100 miles per hour between cafes. The most famous was the Ace Cafe at the southern end of the M1, which was open twenty-four hours a day. The ton-up boy style was practical – they wore checked shirts, turned-up Levi's and winklepickers; a decorated leather motorcycle jacket, pin badges such as an Esso gas man pin, and motorcycle boots. They greased up their hair with Brylcreem and carried a comb in their back pocket. They were often shunned from dance halls because they were seen to be dirty, violent and anti-social, clashing with the mods at a series of Bank Holiday scuffles in the mid-1960s, sparking a moral panic about the youth of the day.

MOD

From its origins amongst a small number of modern jazz fans in London's Soho in the late 1950s, the mod would became the leading UK youth movement by 1964, equally demonised and celebrated in the media. Anything that was cool, modern and quirky was labelled mod; Mary Quant minidresses, the geometric Vidal Sassoon bob, Op Art and André Courrèges space age couture.

Early London mods adored Charlie Parker and Miles Davis – artists who lived music twenty-four hours a day and dressed as sharp as a Wall Street trader. Mods emulated their style of shades, drainpipe trousers and Italian mohair suits, in keeping with Soho's smoky jazz clubs like the Flamingo and Ronnie Scott's. These places sold Coca-Cola rather than beer, but mods found that consuming quantities of amphetamines, blues or purple hearts could keep them going for days.

The Flamingo had originally been a spot for black American GIs, and Geno Washington, who would start up his own band in England in 1965, said: 'We didn't really know anything about the mods at that point but suddenly these kids started showing up wearing sharp Italian suits and long leather coats. Everyone got real sharp man.' This modern jazz fashion in the late 1950s was different from the trad jazz style favoured by middle-class art school students, with their duffel coats and woollen jumpers. Instead, mods drew on the idea of the dandy with an obsessiveness for clean, neat tailoring, creaseless shirts and handmade Italian shoes. Cecil Gee's, a boutique that had originally specialised in zoot suits, was the first retailer to sell Brioni mohair suits imported from Rome, originally with a short boxy jacket known as a 'bum freezer'.

The mod embraced anything European – Jean Paul Sartre, European cinema like Roman Polanski's *Repulsion* or Jean-Luc Godard's *À bout de souffle*, Gauloises cigarettes – and mixed it with an American Ivy League style, including Brooks Brothers' button-down shirts and Harrington jackets with tartan lining. They swapped sculpted Brylcreem hair for a college boy cut or French crop. The French wore dogtooth check, so British mods began to wear it too. They hung out in Italian coffee bars in Soho like the legendary 2i's, where their

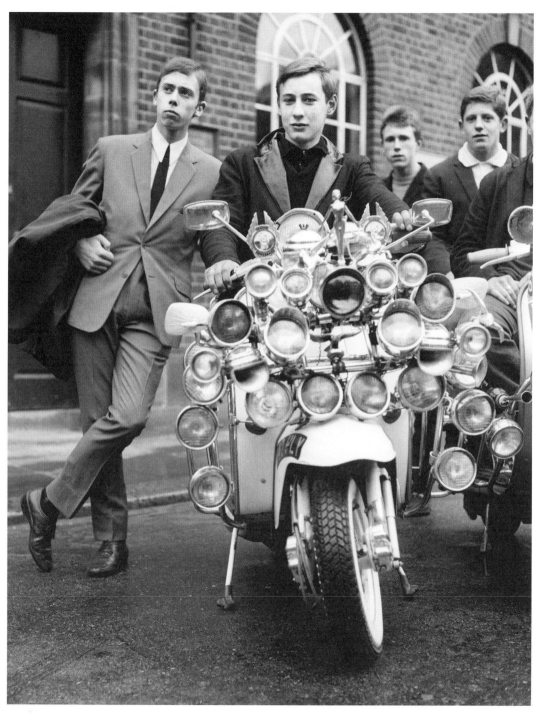

PREVIOUS PAGE Mods in parkas, 1964 LEFT London's Carnaby Street, 1966 ABOVE Mods in Peckham, London, 1964

ABOVE LEFT Assistants at John Stephen boutique, London, 1965 ABOVE RIGHT Young mods window shopping, 1964

imported Gaggia coffee machine made authentic Italian espresso to serve up alongside live music. By embracing these European styles, they achieved the pavement cafe lifestyle before low-cost holidays opened up Europe and allowed widespread travel to the source.

By 1960 Britain had come out of the postwar gloom and a surge in white-collar office work and new technology meant social mobility was possible for most people. Mods had disposable income and higher purchase options to spend on the right clothes, which would go out of fashion in a month, and records,

firstly jazz then obscure rhythm and blues. Richard Shirman of the band the Attack said: 'The coolest thing you could do was walk around the West End of London with the latest LP under your arm.'

Differentiating themselves from the rockers, modernists chose sleek scooters as their mode of transport, instead of greasy motorbikes. They wore American military parka jackets to keep their suits clean and crease free, and would customise their scooters by overloading them with chrome lamps and mirrors, or applying stick-on bullet holes to the fly screen à la James Bond.

Being a mod was about one-upmanship, and the 'faces', the top mods, had the sharpest clothes and the chrome Lambretta TV200 or Vespa GS, while the 'tickets' were followers. Mods didn't have the style section of magazines to dictate what they wore; they set the trends themselves, having their own suits created at Burton's or one of the hundreds of tailors around Hackney and the East End. They would describe to the tailor exactly how they wanted their suit to look, having sketched out the costumes while watching Jean Paul Belmondo films in the cinema. In a *Rave* magazine article in 1964, eighteen-year-old Mick Tanner said: 'Before, tailors used to invent the styles and everyone bought them. Now we invent them and the tailors are going out of their mind trying to keep up. I started wearing crepe, nylon cycling jumpers because they were cool for dancing. All the tickets wanted to know where I got it – but if I told them they'd all be down the shop tomorrow.'

Where previously there were limited styles and colours that men could wear, mods incorporated a riot of hues into their fashion. They would dye their Clarks desert boots, pick up colourful Fred Perry and Ben Sherman shirts, and wear shrink-to-fit Levi's. Some even wore pink denims. Mods shared the values of the Conservatives because they believed in working for a disposal income to afford their consumerist lifestyle. Terence Spencer, who photographed groups of mods in 1964, said: 'I was amazed by the amount of money that the mods would spend on their clothes, and on their hair, and

on their scooters. Remember, we were just coming out of the kind of period when no one was well off.'

Carnaby Street and the King's Road were groundbreaking in offering stylish boutiques where young mods could mix with celebrities such as Mick Jagger. The Small Faces bought their checked shirts, striped suits and basket-weave shoes from shops like Lord John and John Stephen; a young, ambitious Glaswegian designer who sold affordable made-to-measure Italian-style suits and American Ivy Look fashions. His boutiques, including Mod Male, His Clothes and Male West One, were the first to have hip shop assistants modelling the clothes, who, as Stephen himself said, 'just smoke and lean against the wall and put records on.'

Following the success of their anthem 'My Generation', The Who became the mod band to listen to, with their Pop Art sensibility adopting typical British symbols like the Union Jack and the RAF target, giving them an alternative meaning. As the first generation to escape military service, mods wore khaki parka jackets with epaulettes and regimental badges, offending their parents who had experienced the real horror of war. It was similarly revolutionary to turn the sacred Union Jack into a jacket, and when Keith Moon sewed the target badge to a white t-shirt, he started a huge craze. The target would also be used as the symbol for *Ready Steady Go!*, a live Friday night TV programme that brought mod fashion and music into living rooms across the country.

vespa

1964
Bank Holiday battles

John Stephen on
Carnaby Street

Ready Steady Go!

Swinging London

1958   MOD   1963   1966

1957
Flamingo Club opens

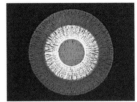

RIGHT Outside the Flamingo Club, London, 1964

Mod girls followed after the boys who would often ignore them or were caught up in their own world of music, style and pills. Writer Nik Cohn recalled one mod who wouldn't have sex at a party 'unless there was a shoe-tree available and a press for his trousers.' Mod girls wore the cropped hair of Jean Seberg or a Juliette Greco long bob, shift dresses and leather coats, while Mary Quant's Bazaar boutique on King's Road created an Italian-inspired modernist look for teenage girls.

The Bank Holiday fights between the mods and rockers in 1964 brought them to the attention of the press as they fought and vandalised their way across the pleasure fronts of Brighton and Margate, while Carnaby Street and the King's Road went into full swing as mod fashion became must-haves. *Time* magazine coined the phrase 'Swinging London' in 1966, and announced in an article that 'the city is alive with birds and Beatles, buzzing with mini-cars

and telly stars, pulsing with half a dozen separate veins of excitement.' But by then the heyday of the mod was already over as LSD and the San Francisco hippie look seeped in and the Beatles psychedelic *Sergeant Pepper* became the album of choice.

The mod style experienced a revival by 1977, led by The Jam's Paul Weller with his spiky mod haircut, three-button suit and Carnaby Street sticker on his guitar. A small mod scene began to thrive with kids in madras jackets, army surplus and mopeds. When *Quadrophenia*, the film based on the Who's rock opera, hit the cinema and told the tale of a young 1960s mod, it brought back a sense of patriotism and nostalgia for clean-living in the midst of the punk and skinhead scene. This mod revival would continue to have strong influence on the 'Cool Britannia' labels like Ben Sherman, Burberry and Paul Smith, and the Britpop scene of the mid-1990s.

SURFER

The surfer lifestyle in the 1960s was a counterculture turned mainstream phenomenon, from Hawaii and California, to Australia and Peru. It was a community that eschewed material possessions in favour of smoking weed, holding beer parties and living hand to mouth on the beaches; an image maintained with Sean Penn's portrayal of Jeff in the 1982 film *Fast Times at Ridgemont High* and the surf gang in *Point Break* in 1991. The romantic lifestyle and endless youthful summers, combined with a celebration of the exoticism of tropical Hawaii and California dreaming, set the scene for a myth of sun and surf.

When the Beach Boys sang in 'Surfin' USA' of 'wearing their baggies, huarache sandals too, a bushy, bushy blonde hairdo', it brought the appeal of casual surf style into the mainstream. Surfers wore loose shirts over 'baggie' shorts, designed to protect from board wax and loose enough to let water circulate; their hair was long, salt-encrusted and sun-bleached.

Beach bums and beach bunnies gathered on the beaches around So-Cal, creating a slang which combined Hawaii surf terms with Valley-speak – the shaka greeting and words like dude, awesome, radical, stoked and gnarly. Cars also brought the opportunity of travelling the Californian coastline to find the best surf spots. The VW campervan and a Pontiac woodie, with panels that could be removed, were perfect for loading up the surfboards and sleeping in the back.

The surfing subculture rejected consumerism for a more spiritual existence, despite the material industry that would build up around it. It was a dedicated way of life – surfers were up at 5 a.m. to catch waves, and would drop everything when someone cried 'surfs up!' The original ten-foot boards made of redwood were also incredibly heavy and only for the devoted. There was cliqueness to the surf culture gangs who looked down on the hodads – beach posers who didn't go near the water.

The Southern California surf scene was inspired by the Hawaiian tradition of *he'e nalu*, or wave sliding, where Kahunas would pray for good surf. After Hawaii was 'discovered' by Captain Cook, the indigenous culture was almost destroyed by traders, settlers and missionaries who tried to do away with sinful native pursuits. By the 1900s, when the first hotel at Waikiki opened, surfing was revived by the beach boys who would perform for tourists, and in their downtime would hang out on the beach and play the ukulele. Honolulu-born George Freeth and Olympic medalist Duke Kahanamoku were both credited with bringing surfing to California, with Freeth giving surf demonstrations at Redondo and Venice in 1907 and Kahanamoku spreading out to Australia with a demonstration at Freshwater Beach in New South Wales in 1915.

In the 1930s Hawaii became a holiday paradise, and with beach and leisurewear becoming more popular, in 1938 *Vogue* magazine featured a surf girl on their cover, riding the waves in a Hawaiian print swimsuit. Surf culture really gained more ground after the Second World War as a way of bringing back leisure time and the idea of the endless summer, where young people could sunbathe and play in the surf without a care for responsibilities. In 1959 Sandra Dee played surfer girl *Gidget*, a portmanteau of girl and midget, and by the 1960s it had exploded into all aspects of American culture. Radios blasted out the California sound of Dick Dale, the Beach Boys and the Surfaris, which incorporated Hawaiian-inspired sounds. Frankie Avalon starred in dozens of beach movies in the 1960s including *Muscle Beach Party* and *Beach Blanket Bingo*.

California surfer Phil Edwards, who named the Banzai pipeline in Ohau, said in 1966: 'When it started on the Coast not too many years ago, it was a form of rebellion. You see, people spend too much of their time today being spoon-fed by organised society . . . sure, surfing was born of rebellion, and there was a certain amount of freestyle beer drinking and beach wrecking when it all caught on. You must remember that all kids are hell-raisers to a

certain extent. But in surfing – as in anything else – talent will inevitably rise to the top.'

Dale Velzy opened the first surf shop in the United States in Manhattan Beach in 1950 and by 1960 he was the world's biggest surfboard manufacturer, creating them by hand from raw lengths of wood and later polyurethane. 'There would be no surf business without Dale Velzy,' said *Surfer* magazine, 'and hence no surf life as we know it. He was the first to put a name on a surfboard, the first to sponsor a surfer, the first to open a surf shop and the first to print a surf company t-shirt.' John Severson, the founder of *Surfer* magazine, developed a style of surf art, photographs and footage that captured the lifestyle, the rebellious innovations and death defying skills involved in tackling huge waves. He lived it himself in the 1960s, where he and his gang 'could usually get in on a pot of rice and beans being cooked on the beach, scratch up beer money by exchanging some empties, maybe sell some paintings to tourists.'

Surf clothes had a tropical influence with Hawaiian flower prints like the palm leaf or frangipani. Aloha shirts were originally created in Hawaii for Chinese immigrant workers, where island motifs were hand-painted on to tapa cloth. By 1936 designs were printed on to silk and mass-marketed to tourists flocking to the islands for vacation, and who wanted a shirt with palm trees, surfers, leis and hula dancers to bring back home.

Waikiki Beach by the mid-1960s was attracting thousands of young people over summer, including students, hippies and beach bums looking for the surf lifestyle. In a profile in *Sports Illustrated* in 1967, it was described as 'a massive bikini-clad protest against work, war, marriage and worry.' They noted how 'the girl must wear a bikini, must be deeply tanned, must be beautiful and must never, never, for God's sake, be fat. Preferably, she should have long, silken hair, but short hair is being accepted now. If she has long hair, she must never, as she once did long ago – like last summer – keep her hairbrush stuck into the hip of her bikini . . .' Boys, the article said, should never wear new swim trunks, must be toned and bronzed, must never have an armed forces haircut, and if 'he is really hip, he will wear a pair of $1.50 plaid underwear shorts instead of a swimsuit, and they will be slightly faded.'

The outdoor California surf industry had an effect on mainstream fashion by the mid-1960s, offering an escape from the confines of the button-down shirt suit, which was still the fashion staple for men. '"Breezy" does it for the steadily growing California men's and boys' apparel industry,' wrote the *New York Times* in 1964. 'Short-sleeved sweaters, blue Levi's, denims, casual sports shoes,

TARKENTON Part 2
Sports Illustrated
JULY 24, 1967 40 CENTS
THE SUMMER SURFERS INVADE HAWAII

1901
Moana hotel on
Waikiki opens

Wetsuit invented

'Surfin' USA' by the Beach Boys

1915

1952

SURFER

1963

1969

Duke Kahanamoku
visits Australia

Jack O'Neill's Ocean
Beach surf shop opens

Quicksilver founded

TOP LEFT Malibu beach, Californa, 1970 BOTTOM LEFT The Beach Boys in their Pendleton shirts, Los Angeles, 1962

terrycloth swim trunks, casual jackets, bright sports coats with contrasting slacks, cabana swim-and-lounge sets, and his-and-hers swim wear.'

In Australia, surfing developed into an all-encompassing culture where every coastal town had its surf club. In 1963 the *New York Times* reported on the surf subculture taking over Australia, with its own language, heroes and music, and where 20,000 surfboards were registered in Sydney alone. 'The city belongs once more to the tribe of bronze boys and golden girls, at Maroubra, Bondi, Dee Why, Collaroy, Curl Curl and Narrabeen they again engage in the rituals of the surf cult.' Just like in California, where the 'bushy, bushy blonde hair' was the surf look, in Sydney 'a flash of bright yellow hair identifies the teller or bellboy as a member of the tribe. Prolonged exposure to the sun can bleach hair this colour, but the dedicated tribesman helps the process along with peroxide, lemon juice or even sink cleaner.' They also reportedly fought with the inland rocker gangs, echoing the macho 'brotherhood' culture of the Bra Boys gang of Maroubra beach, forty years later.

While surfing clothing companies began as cottage industries in the 1970s, founded by surfers for surfers, brands such as Quicksilver, Billabong and Rip Curl became huge businesses, with logo t-shirts, boardshorts and neoprene that could be worn in the city. Suburban Australians particularly liked the city beach bum aesthetic in the 1980s and *Time* magazine reported total surfwear sales in 1986 hit the $1 billion mark.

HIPPIE

Whether it was boho style, psychedelia or hippie chic, the fashions that came from an anti-consumerist counterculture in the 1960s have had a lasting impact on the way we dress. Hippie style was loose fitting and natural, with Indian and African cottons, tie-dye, flowers, beads and denims. It harked back to Art Nouveau design, with its organic look inspired by nature which acted as a symbol of protest against society's greed.

The hippies emerged in 1965 in Haight-Ashbury, San Francisco, with a similar language and philosophy to the beats, but instead of dark clothes, shades and goatees, they displayed their individuality with long hair, folky fashions and psychedelic designs.

It was a folk music-inspired social consciousness, with a turned-on, tuned-out, dropped-out ethos. Hippies created their own open communities which encouraged the sexual revolution. They opposed nuclear war, Vietnam and the damage being done to the environment. Psychedelic drugs expanded their consciousness and their creative output depicted their ethos of peace, love, freedom and standing up to the Man.

The name 'hippie' was first used in a 1965 article by Michael Fallon describing the bohemian groups who moved from North Beach to Haight-Ashbury – still with the counterculture attitude of the hipster beat poet. Hippie culture can be traced back to the German movement *Der Wandervogal* at the turn of the twentieth century, which promoted folk music, paganism and organic, healthy foods. Many of the Germans who settled in California brought this alternative lifestyle with them and opened health food stores to promote it. It was adopted by the Nature Boys, a group in the California desert who celebrated a back-to-nature lifestyle. Eden Ahbez wrote the song 'Nature Boy' which became a hit with Nat King Cole's recording in 1948. In *On the Road* Kerouac noted that while passing through Los Angeles in the summer of 1947 he saw 'an occasional Nature Boy saint in beard and sandals.'

PREVIOUS PAGE Hippies at the Hyde Park Love-In, 1967 ABOVE Elysian Park Love-In, Los Angeles, 1967

While the hippie culture also grew from the Venice coffee houses and clubs of Sunset Strip, it was at Haight-Ashbury that it all came together with those formerly part of the beat scene. Around 1963 Allen Ginsberg, who would become a prominent voice of the anti-war movement, and Neal Cassady, who lived in one of the communes in the cheap Victorian apartments, formed a collective called the Merry Pranksters. The group included Ken Kesey, who participated in the CIA-sponsored LSD trials, Mountain Girl and Wavy Gravy, and travelled across America by psychedelic-painted school bus, giving out LSD-laced Kool-aid and marijuana to those they encountered. Tom Wolfe documented this in *The Electric Kool-Aid Acid Test*, describing the hippie look as 'Jesus Christ strung out hair, Indian beads, Indian headbands, donkey beads, temple bells,

amulets, mandalas, God's eyes, fluorescent vests, unicorn horns, Errol Flynn dueling shirts.'

Communes sprang up across the country, including Hog Farm and the Diggers, a community guerrilla group in Haight-Ashbury who wanted to create a free society. The Red Dog Experience at a saloon in Nevada in 1965 was one of the first free hippie music festivals, where the Grateful Dead, Jefferson Airplane and others played together. Singers like Janis Joplin and Joni Mitchell, with her flowing hair, bare feet, floral maxi-dresses and ethnic sweaters, roused protest amongst those disaffected by US involvement in Vietnam and by their country's nuclear programme.

In January 1967, the Human Be-In in Golden Gate Park sparked the Summer of Love on the west coast with love-ins, be-ins, mind altering drugs

ABOVE LEFT Hippie, 1969 ABOVE RIGHT Ken Kesey and the Merry Pranksters' psychedelic bus, Woodstock, 1969

and flower power. With the Monterey Pop Festival in June of that same year, the counterculture went mainstream, and around 15,000 young people flocked to Haight-Ashbury from across America. The Summer of Love was about flower power, and skin painted with bright, swirling acid-trip colours – everyone wanted to go to San Francisco with a flower in their hair, like Scott McKenzie's hit song.

In July 1967 *The Times* cynically reported, 'The mind boggles at the thought of so much long hair and bare feet, so much incense and marijuana and LSD . . . it's virtually impossible in the Haight-Ashbury to walk a hundred paces without being accosted by hippie beggars, bumping into gawking tourists from Iowa or tripping over youths who lie about on the sidewalk for hours, twanging their guitars and tootling their flutes.'

By 1967, the fashion-conscious in the UK were adopting psychedelia, replacing the Mod fashion of Swinging London. Hair was grown longer and hippie style replaced the more streamlined, modernist look. The hippie-lite trend was popular with baby boomers as a way of buying into this counterculture without living on communes.

The Afghan coat was a symbol of the hippie's Eastern gaze. It became a fashion item when worn by the Beatles – made from sheep or goatskin, sourced in the Ghazni province of Afghanistan, and imported into London. As hippies turned to the East for inspiration, designers soon followed suit, with clothes for the jet set hippie – flowing dresses, long romantic sleeves and kaftans. Socialites Anita Pallenberg and Talitha Getty were the boho style icons who holidayed in Morocco, and wore

ABOVE Outside the Hung On You boutique, King's Road, London, 1967 RIGHT Hyde Park Festival, London, 1970

1963
Vietnam War escalates

Merry Pranksters road trip
1964

HIPPIE

1967

Woodstock
1969

Human Be-In,
Golden Gate Park

Laura Ashley founded

1970
Isle of Wight Festival

The Beatles'
*Sergeant Pepper's
Lonely Hearts Club Band*

designer hippie dresses by Emilio Pucci, in swirling psychedelic silk, and Ossie Clark and Celia Birtwell, with their bold flower prints.

The 1966 Aubrey Beardsley exhibition at the Victoria & Albert Museum tapped in to the Art Nouveau-inspired psychedelia as evident in posters for festivals and rock album covers, which blended Art Nouveau with Victoriana, in acid-trip colours. This style had flourished in San Francisco with artists like Rick Griffin, Stanley Mouse and Alton Kelley, and in turn inspired the designs of Barbara Hulanicki at Biba whose wildly popular clothes used luxurious velvets and brocade. Laura Ashley, whose first London shop opened in 1967, was nostalgically pastoral, with floral dresses and Victorian high-neck blouses, embracing the back-to-nature ethos.

The Beatles had plunged into psychedelia with *Sergeant Pepper*, and they made a pilgrimage to India to see their guru, Maharishi Mahesh Yogi, an experience which inspired the *White Album*. Mia Farrow, Mick Jagger, Donovan and the Beach Boys were also drawn to the ashram in Rishikesh, India. John Lennon and Yoko Ono with their long hair, white suits and bed-ins represented a new generation who wanted more than the 1950s ideal, and worked

tirelessly to disseminate the anti-war message, holding their first bed-in in March 1969.

At the Hyde Park Love-in in July 1967 activist Steve Abrams declared: 'Make love, do anything you want, we are here to be happy,' as the crowd danced, some naked, many high. There were free concerts and love-ins that continued across the country, and in 1970 the Isle of Wight Festival attracted 400,000 people, marked by what would be the last performance by Jimi Hendrix.

But the hippie dream was fading as many of those living in Haight-Asbury became desolate, malnourished and addicted to drugs, and by the end of 1967 the original hippies had become disillusioned with what they saw. The widespread media coverage soon turned to a moral panic around their pro-drug stance and anti-work ethic. Hippies began to be depicted as dangerous with their wild lifestyle of sex and drugs, as in B-movie shockers including *Psych-Out* and *The Love-Ins*.

In the US, in August 1969, the counterculture came to a head with Woodstock. 500,000 people descended on Bethel, New York, to hear the Grateful Dead, Janis Joplin, Crosby Stills and Nash, Jimi Hendrix and the Who, spreading an anti-Vietnam War

John Paul Getty, Jr. and wife Talitha, wearing Moroccan kaftans at their house in Marrakech, 1970

message. But the movement turned on itself with the arrests of the Manson family and the Altamont Free Concert in California in December 1969, when Hell's Angels hired as security killed a concert goer.

Hippie culture continued throughout the 1970s, as the original hippies left San Francisco to create homesteads in New Mexico, New York and Colorado. In Britain New Age travellers celebrated paganism at Stonehenge, and took off in VW 'peace' campervans on the hippie trail from Europe to India, settling in Goa where the psychedelic legacy would continue with the trance scene in the 1990s. The hippie subculture heavily influenced popular culture by encouraging Eastern philosophy, healthy eating and vegetarianism – an ethos that is still evident with the popularity of yoga, music festivals like Glastonbury and Coachella and the widespread growth of the health food industry.

RUDEBOY

Rudeboy style was born in the streets of Kingston, Jamaica, amongst the swaying palm trees and heat of the shanty towns, in the years leading up to and immediately following the country's independence from Britain in 1962.

The rudeboys or rudies were the hustlers and young rebels who acted out violent and anti-social behavior while distinctively dressed in sharp mohair suits, thin ties, pork-pie hats and shades. Trousers were cut short, while vibrant socks or a loosened tie would add a burst of colour. It was the look of an urbane 'soul brother'. As sartorial influences came from the gangster and wild west fashions depicted in the Hollywood movies that were so popular in Jamaica, the rudeboys often took on a Robin Hood persona in the midst of rising unemployment and struggles. Herbie Miller, curator of the Jamaica Music Museum told the *New York Times*: 'Any early rudeboys were seen as strugglers who turned to violence and crime.' It was the 'idea of liberation for the common man: if you can't get jobs, if education and healthcare is poor, you resist by turning against the system . . . with language, how one wore clothes or challenged the traditional European style of dress.'

The Kingston fashion was to wear your Sunday best on a daily basis, a sharp, tailored look topped with a rakish hat. Jamaica had a more urban flavour than other Caribbean islands, preferring the latest African American music to merengue, and the dance halls became a heaving, vibrant space to hear the latest music on massive sound systems.

In Jamaica's 1950s dancehalls it was cheaper for organisers to hire a sound system than pay for a band, and it was where everyone could gather to hear a record without the expense of buying it themselves. The sound systems were made up of huge amplifiers and loudspeakers, designed to play in the open air as dance parties would take place in Kingston, and out in the smaller towns. Dick Hebdige in *Subculture: The Meaning of Style*, wrote that 'to a community hemmed in on all sides by discrimination, hostility, suspicion and blank incomprehension, the sound-system came to represent, particularly for the young, a precious inner sanctum, uncontaminated by alien influences, a black heart beating back to Africa on a steady pulse of dub.'

The DJs ruled the dance floors, and those who invested in the loudest, baddest systems would also take pride in the uniqueness of their sounds. There would be sound clashes, where two systems competed, and prominent rivals included Prince Buster, Duke Reid, who ran the Treasure Isle Liquor Store in Kingston, and Clement Seymour Dodd, known as Sir Coxsone. They would travel to the States to collect American jazz and rhythm and blues and then hide the identity of obscure records by covering up the label so their rivals couldn't get hold of it. But the rock'n'roll that was coming from America wasn't hard and fast enough to satisfy Jamaican tastes, and they began to develop homegrown talent.

Orange Street, known as Beat Street, in Kingston was an area of outdoor dance 'lawns' where well-dressed Jamaicans in the 1940s gathered to show off their flash jitterbug moves, with the men in their best suits and the women in full skirts and petticoats. It was here, on Beat Street, that a distinctly Jamaican sound of ska and rocksteady would be developed by 1959, amidst the vibrancy of record shops and recording studios.

The Duke Reid-produced single 'Rough and Tuff', by Stranger Cole, was said to be the first rudeboy anthem, representing a brewing atmosphere in Kingston as Jamaica gained independence in 1962. It brought a new self-confidence, reflected by young men looking up to the bad-boy figure in Hollywood who was invincible and wore his smart suit as a uniform. As Desmond Dekker sang in 'Shanty Town', 'Dem rudeboys out on probation, them a rude when them come up to town.'

In 1963 eighteen-year-old Bob Marley and his band the Wailers, originally the Wailing Rudeboys, released their first single 'Simmer Down', on the legendary Studio One label in Jamaica. The lyrics aimed to calm his mother, who was concerned about her son being in with the Trench Town crowds. He spoke directly to the rudeboys, who were well known for their violent behavior: 'Simmer down, oh control your temper. Simmer down, for the battle will be hotter.' Rudeboys soon became hired thugs offering protection for producers like Duke Reid, and enforcers for the country's two political parties. It seemed the only way out of the shanty town was through music or through crime.

While ska began with a frantic jazz beat, over time it slowed down and went deeper, becoming what is known as reggae, giving a voice to the oppressed Jamaican people. Reggae became associated with Rastafarians, with a more political and spiritual message.

Chuka and Dubem, London, 1979

In the 1950s West Indians began immigrating to Britain, pictured arriving off the boats in their finest suits and smart coats expectant of a country they had fought for during the Second World War. By the mid-sixties half a million had settled in London and Birmingham. They rented houses from slum landlords in Brixton, Notting Hill and Ladbroke Grove in London, where the Jamaican influx brought a taste of home with cafes serving up curried goat and rice, and the sounds of ska drifting through illegal drinking dens to break up the cold, staid environments they found themselves in. They

ABOVE LEFT Gaz Mayall, London, 1980s ABOVE RIGHT Pauline Black at Andy's Records, 1980

brought with them ska and rocksteady, and the look of the rudeboy, which proved captivating to the style-conscious mods.

Former mod Ian Hebditch said the rudeboys 'wore their trousers shorter than we would wear them, with socks showing. Also they brought the idea of never doing your tie up. You always had a button undone. The influence was seen in the way they wore their clothes which was with a kind of arrogance that the mods had as well.'

Island Records and Blue Beat began selling larger numbers of Jamaican imports from 1962, and in London they could be sourced at West Indian food shops, Portobello Road market stalls, or heard in dingy, reefer-smoking clubs like the Roaring Twenties. Desmond Dekker's 1967 hit '007 (Shanty Town)' was a surprise success in Britain as it was about the troubles in Jamaica following student

riots. By the late 1960s, many of the rudeboys turned to a Rastafari way of life, growing their hair into dreads.

In 1979 the Two Tone record label revived ska by giving it a punk edge through bands like the Specials, the Selecter and Madness. They kicked off the UK ska revival with 'The Prince', a tribute to Prince Buster and Orange Street, while the name Two Tone came from a desire to create a multicultural harmony in Britain. Over its two-year chart domination from 1979 to 1981, Two Tone offered an alternative to the skinhead style that had adopted rudeboy ska elements but had become infused with racism and football hooliganism. The Two Tone style adapted the Jamaican rudeboy look with tonic suits, pork-pie hats, button-down Ben Sherman shirts and loafers worn with white socks. The signature design for Two Tone was a black and

Ska on Beat Street, Kingston

Rastafarian movement

1959   1962   **RUDEBOY**   1963   1965

Jamaican
independence

1979
Two Tone revival

Bob Marley's 'Simmer Down'

RIGHT Ska and Two Tone fans in the bar at a Selecter gig, 1979

white check with the logo of a rudeboy, known as Walt Jabsco. It represented the racial unity of a mixed crowd of people who would come to gigs, despite the threat of violence from ska-loving skinheads. The Two Tone fans would wear a uniform of black and white clothing, or Italian suits with obligatory shades. It was a style that fitted with the cool look of the *Blues Brothers*, released in 1980.

Pauline Black was the lead singer of the Selecter and poster girl for ska, changing her name from Vickers to Black as a statement of her identity. After forming the band, she toned down her 1970s afro and fashioned a feminine rudeboy style, buying most of her clothes from second-hand shops. She recounted in her autobiography that she chose beige sta-Prest trousers which stopped an inch above her ankle, Ben Sherman shirts, 'a double-breasted jacket made of shiny grey material' and 'a pair of black penny loafers at a downmarket shoe shop, Ravel. White socks took up the spatial slack between the trouser bottoms and my shoes.' She finished the look with a pair of fake Raybans and 'a dove-grey fedora with a dark grey ribbon hatband'; the hat that would become her signature.

Two Tone experienced further revivals with a ska scene thriving in the United States in the 1980s and 1990s, producing bands like No Doubt and the Mighty Mighty Bosstones. In recent years the rudeboy style has been reinvigorated by those looking for a smart, swaggering look to convey a sense of smooth urban style. But it lacks the historical context of the original rudeboys, born from political upheaval and inspired by American wild west rebels.

SKINHEAD

'The sight of cropped heads and the sound of heavy boots entering the midnight Wimpy bar or dance hall is the real cause for sinking feelings in the pit of the stomach,' said *Melody Maker* in 1969.

When people talk about skinheads, they think of the National Front and thuggish youths with shaven heads. But skinheads originally came from groups of harder, more violent mods, dressing in a gang uniform style inspired by ska music and the West Indian community, and which played up to their working-class status. They were described by the *Telegraph* in 1968 as dressing in 'hillbilly fashion', and by George Melly as 'a pack of weasels squeaking for blood'.

As the mods grew older, they moved towards the fashion for psychedelia which arrived in Britain around 1966. But a splinter group of hard mods, those known as the 'Fred Perry brigade', who were more violent, went in a different direction – they did not like the middle-class hippies who rejected work despite being funded by their parents. While the hippies were tuning in and dropping out, life on council estates didn't seem so great.

There was a threatening, clipped neatness to their look. Hair was cropped, but not the shaved look of later years, boots were heavy-duty and polished, and Levi's were held up by braces. As one skinhead, Chris Brick, recounted: 'Once I had this clean look all poverty dropped off me. It was gone. I became somebody.'

They wore the basic elements of the mod – a button-down Ben Sherman shirt with stripes or in bright colours, or a red, white and blue checked Brutus shirt with short sleeves and a Harrington jacket. Fred Perry tennis shirts, advertised with the slogan 'Shirt by Fred. Nuff said,' could be worn in football colours, with piping on the collar and sleeves. Abercrombie jackets were often too expensive but cheaper alternatives could be made up at Burton's. Early skinheads wore red-tag 501 Levi jeans, or Lee and Wrangler if they were outside of London, and they would soak them in a bucket of bleach to get them looking faded and used. In the back pocket was a steel comb with a sharpened end, perfect for sticking someone.

Added to this was the look of a Jamaican rudeboy, coming from their appreciation of West Indies ska music. White mods would regularly visit the illicit drinking dens to hear the latest sounds coming from Jamaica. Many of the black kids wore a rudeboy style, and this in turn inspired the white mods to wear suits shortened at the ankle and sleeve, a rakish trilby and well-polished shoes. Gary Kingham, an original skinhead, recalled: 'The whole scene was highly influenced by black culture, the haircut, the length of our trousers, the walk, the dances, some of the talk, and of course the music. Much of it was copied from the rudeboy style.'

Tony Cousins, who founded the Creole booking agency, remembered how Desmond Dekker inspired the white kids to dress. 'When we brought Desmond Dekker over we gave him a suit, but he insisted that the bottom six inches of the trousers should be cut off. Then the kids began to follow him, they rolled up their trousers and had their hair cut short.'

Like the rudeboys, skinheads held their jeans in place with braces, so they could pull them up to their waist and above the ankles, to show off their boots. It was these bovver boots, heavy-duty enough to cause 'bother' when kicking someone, that demonstrated how tough they were and gave them the nickname of 'boot boys'. As long as they had the boots, they could call themselves a skinhead. The bigger the boots, the better, and some wore theirs a size bigger or exposed the steel-toe caps to look even harder. When Symarip's 'Skinhead Moonstop' was released in 1969, it defined the stomping style of dancing that the skinheads would do.

The hair wasn't as important as the boot, and despite their name, it wasn't necessary to have a number one haircut. Others had short back and sides, a shaved in parting or an American army style crew cut. They grew sideburns if they could, as it made them look older, wiser and harder.

While the style of the skinhead came from mods and rudeboys, football played a big part in their development. Interest in the sport amongst young people spiked following England's World Cup success in 1966, and with it came a more organised type of football violence. The football boot boys emerged on the terraces around 1967 and rival gangs dressed in jeans, shirts and steel-capped boots, which became a weapon in themselves. The police took to lining the boot boys up against the wall, insisting they remove their boots and throw them in a pile until their rival gang had got far enough away. It was only after steel-toes were classed as an offensive weapon in 1969, to cut down on football violence, that Doc Martens, often cherry red, became popular. If brogues were worn, they would be black, brown or oxblood in colour.

The pervading concept of a skinhead is a racist, and while their anger and aggression was based around class and territory, anti-immigration sentiment was being stirred up in the media. By the late 1960s thousands of disaffected skinheads were becoming a de facto youth group for the National Front, taking out their aggression on Asian communities who were easier to bully. Hippies were also fair game as they were considered by skins to be dirty scroungers.

When 30,000 students in London marched against the Vietnam War in October 1968 the skins turned up, not to offer support, but to mock the protesters. Skinheads and hippies also clashed at the free Rolling Stones concert in Hyde Park in July 1969, where Hell's Angels had been paid to keep the 250,000 crowd in check. Oz magazine, a hippie journal, reported: 'The spikeys, or brushcuts,

1965
Hard mods

England win World Cup
1966

SKINHEAD

Steel-toe boots
banned in the UK
1969

Suedeheads
1970

1971
Stanley Kubrick's
A Clockwork Orange

OPPOSITE Young skinhead couple, 1980

are summer's new dumb terrorists in jeans, braces and thick leather boots. With sharpened aluminum combs to match they have already wrecked one major free concert.'

Skinheads became cult figures on film in 1971 when Stanley Kubrick's controversial *A Clockwork Orange* heavily referenced the style of the skinheads. The droogs wore thin braces, rakish hats, heavy boots and canes with blades, and spoke in the hybrid of cockney and Slavic created by Anthony Burgess in the original book.

Female skinheads adopted the boys' masculine look of Levi's, Ben Sherman, braces and brogues, but wore a fringe at the front of their shaved head. They wore permanent press button-down blouses, often had numerous piercings up their ear, and in the 1970s their style was a feminist reaction to how beauty was defined. There were no high heels or time-consuming make-up for them. There was also the smoothie girl style. She wore a Trevira suit with short skirt, brogue shoes, and hair that was feather cut or in the style of Jean Shrimpton.

By 1970 skinheads became known as suede-heads, as they wore their hair a little longer and, fed up with hassle from the police, softened their look.

They wore brogues instead of boots, and a Crombie overcoat or Harrington jacket over their Fred Perry shirt. While few could afford real mohair or tonic suits, they wore suits in lighter shades of brown and blue, or even in houndstooth or the Prince of Wales check. Some suedeheads even began wearing a bowler hat and carrying an umbrella – the sharpened metal points were useful for fighting. Sometimes a single black driving glove was worn – the origin of this attributed alternatively as a homage to the black power salute, a protection when dropping on the dancefloor to soul music, or to convince people they drove a flash sports car.

By 1977, street punks heralded the return of skinheads – a new breed who used exaggerated style for shock value. Their hair was completely shaven, boots were fully exposed with short trousers, while facial tattoos even became fashionable. 'Oi!' was the sound of the new skinhead, a rebel cry against the early years of Thatcher's Britain, and with it came racism and uncompromising violence. To counteract the racism of the skinhead, a group called SHARP (Skinheads Against Racial Prejudice) was set up to demonstrate that without Jamaican culture, skinheads would not exist.

HIP HOP

Hip hop style grew out of a seven-mile radius in the South Bronx in the early 1970s to become a billion dollar industry by the mid-1990s. Hip hop combined the four elements of DJing, MCing, graffiti writing and breakdancing, where the fashion was about being fly and fresh.

In 1970, the Bronx was a place of poverty and unemployment and the arson capital of the United States. It was home to Puerto Rican and African American youth gangs like Savage Skulls and Black Spades who dressed like Hell's Angels or Peter Fonda and Dennis Hopper in *Easy Rider*, with cut-off denims, military belts, black boots and jackets emblazoned with skull and crossbones. Unlike the late 1950s doo-wop gangs in their smart, sharp silk jackets, these gangs in their 'outlaw' style were rough and threatening as they fought each other and declared war against drug dealers. 'They feel we aren't people, you know, that the colours make us different. But that's the only way we can make a point and make people know we are here,' a Black Spade was quoted as saying in the *New York Times*, revealing the colour patch on his denim jacket.

Similar to creating individual fashions with custom-made jackets, DJing allowed something new to be created from limited means. In the absence of instruments, a turntable became a tool for developing phenomenal skills, such as scratching, while adapting the music they had, from James Brown's funk to songs like 'Apache' by the Shadows. Disco was the current black sound, but its fashion of excess was not relatable to life in the Bronx. It wasn't conceivable to imagine tough street gangs donning disco style. Instead they created their own parties, running their sound systems on power from tapping into lampposts. By 1974 the DJ with the biggest and loudest sound system was DJ Kool Herc. He borrowed the disco technique of using two turntables, and as the dancers went wild at instrumental sections, he developed a way to play only the instrumental breaks – keeping them on a continuous loop – an innovation that would be the foundation of hip hop.

PREVIOUS PAGE LL Cool J and E Love, Queen's, New York, 1986 RIGHT Members of the Bronx Black Magic gang who rejected use of hardcore drugs and tried to take positive action for their neighbourhood

HIP HOP • 109

More block parties sprung up around the Bronx, and it was a former gang member, Afrika Bambaataa, who created Zulu Nation as a way to stop gang violence, instead channeling expression through music and dance. At every party the breakdancers, or 'b-boys', would show off their considerable moves which had been practised in parks and street corners, earning battle scars from broken glass on the ground. The DJ would toast the crowd, hyping the dancers with phrases like, 'to the beat' and 'b-boys, are you ready?'

Crazy Legs, founder of Bronx group Rock Steady Crew, who toured the world and featured in the 1983 film *Flashdance*, said: 'It was our outlet and our way of expressing ourselves and showing our individuality, our character, our strength and our attitude.'

Gangs and the violence associated with them began to disappear from around 1973, as crisp b-boy fashion took over. Followers wore straight-legged Lee jeans, a spray-painted jacket, shell-toe Adidas Superstar sneakers with the laces starched or removed completely (a reference to serving time in prison), caps and tank tops. Being fresh was incredibly important – meaning fresh out the box, brand new. They adapted the limited clothes they had, such as customising the baseball cap by wearing it to the side or back to front. Wearing a flatcap was a link with working class origins, while wearing the baseball cap twisted the concept of leisuretime and

sportswear being a preserve of the wealthy, as it had been up until the 1960s. The fashion for Kangols, a beret manufactured for the army, came from the Vietnam vets who returned home in the 1970s, wearing their berets with pride.

As noted in *Stylin': African American Expressive Culture*, 'When they have space to do so, African American men and women, particularly the young, had often fashioned for themselves a distinctive and visually arresting appearance.'

When cassette tapes of the DJ sets of Kool Herc, Afrika Bambaataa, and Grandmaster Flash and the Furious Five circulated around Brooklyn and Queens, hip hop began to spread from its original source and into the clubs of Harlem. In 1979 Sugarhill Gang's 'Rapper's Delight' reached the top of the charts while with 'Planet Rock', which fused hip hop and Kraftwerk-inspired electronica, Bambaataa became a founding father of hip hop as well as house music.

The other element of early hip hop was graffiti, where writing a tag was like planting a flag. Graffiti artists covered industrial, brick and metal surfaces with bright, tropical colours that responded to civil rights, psychedelia and even colour TV. It was a risky and dangerous business as these mysterious, legendary figures scaled down into the subways and service stops armed with spraypaint and markers. In 1973 *New York* magazine called it, 'the first genuine teenage street culture since the fifties.'

These painted subway trains entered into Manhattan, attracting the attention of the downtown art scene. Commercial galleries commissioned graffiti exhibitions and major museum curators snapped them up. Jean-Michel Basquiat, using the tag Samo, would go from homelessness to international art stardom. Lee Quinones and Fab Five Freddy of the Fab Five Crew created political messages and replicated Andy Warhol's Campbell's soup can over an entire car. Lee and Freddy would help hip hop collide with New York's downtown punk scene when they appeared in Blondie's 'Rapture' video in 1981, wearing the hip hop b-boy street style.

London Blitz kid Ruza Blue started a hip hop club night called Wheels of Steel at punk club Negril and then the Roxy. It attracted a hip crowd of new-wave Madonna types in lacey bras, punks with green hair and b-boys in Kangols and bubble jackets who would be the focus of punk girl attention for their athletic spins and twists on the dancefloor. While both punk and hip hop fashion was about customising, they were diametrically opposite. Punks wore torn t-shirts, but b-boys ensured they had perfect creases in their jeans.

Music journalist David Hershkovits, who observed Jazzy Jay and Freddy polishing their trainers with a toothbrush at the Roxy, said: 'Here were these guys from the ghettos coming out and showing everyone how to dress, how to be fresh, how to be clean, how to have it together – whether it was the way you did your dance or your graffiti or your rapping or your DJing, it was all style.'

It was Run DMC who brought street style to MTV, as the first hip hop band that crossed over into the rock scene with their guitar riffs, leathers and rebellious persona. Their white Adidas worn without laces were shown in close-up for their 'Walk This Way' video, and as they toured across the country they saw the crowds were all dressed like them in tracksuits and Adidas. During a performance of their track 'My Adidas', the crowds would hold up their own sneakers and this mass worship, which was more about a way of life than a sneaker, led to Run DMC being signed as the face of the brand.

Coming from this punk and hip hop scene, the Beastie Boys formed in 1981 with a teenage delinquent sound, and wearing the downtown look of baseball caps, skater shorts and high-tops with the tongue sticking out. Band member Mike D wore a huge VW badge around his neck, making fun of the trend for excess jewellery, but encouraging car vandalism around the world as fans stole the badge to emulate his look.

While the East Coast developed the original hip hop style, the ghettos of Los Angeles brought gangsta rap to public consciousness with Compton's

1990s
Hip hop goes global

Bronx block parties begin
1973

1979

HIP HOP

Run DMC and Adidas
1986

1969
Adidas Superstar
shoe goes on sale

B-boy style

Sugarhill Gang's 'Rapper's
Delight' released

TOP LEFT DJ Run, Jam Master Jay and D.M.C of Run DMC, 1988
BOTTOM LEFT Hip hop street style

NWA and Ice-T, shocking America with a violent depiction of drugs, police brutality and misogyny. The Compton style became the pervading image of hip hop. Trousers were worn low, without a belt (like prisoners who would have their belts removed when they entered jail), and would sport bandanas and baseball caps to the side or backwards.

Designer labels were always a part of the aspirational side of hip hop, and in the 1980s Ralph Lauren had become the sought-after brand by the Lo-Life gang in Crown Heights, Brooklyn, who worshiped the Polo logo and dressed exclusively in the waspy brand. By 1992 they had branched into Guess, Nautica, Tommy Hilfiger and Fila, emulating hip hop stars. 'They gave a new reading to his class/race code,' wrote the *Face* magazine in 1992. 'These B-boys were appropriating ruling class style and parading it with a sardonic grin.' One member of the Lo-Life crew was quoted as saying, 'We're saying fuck you to this rich, white millionaire.'

The group Public Enemy brought a heavily politicised message of black power to their music, and as their message and style reached the public, symbols of black pride became popular again, particularly traditional African patterned clothing in red, black and green. Queen Latifah paid tribute to Africa with her Nefertiti dreadlocks and bold African prints, and Salt-N-Pepa wore wide pants and bright colours, and big, bold jewellery.

As hip hop stars gained success and money, it would turn into an industry of Scarface-inspired suits, fistfuls of gold around fingers and necks, and with a continued appreciation of fresh sportswear.

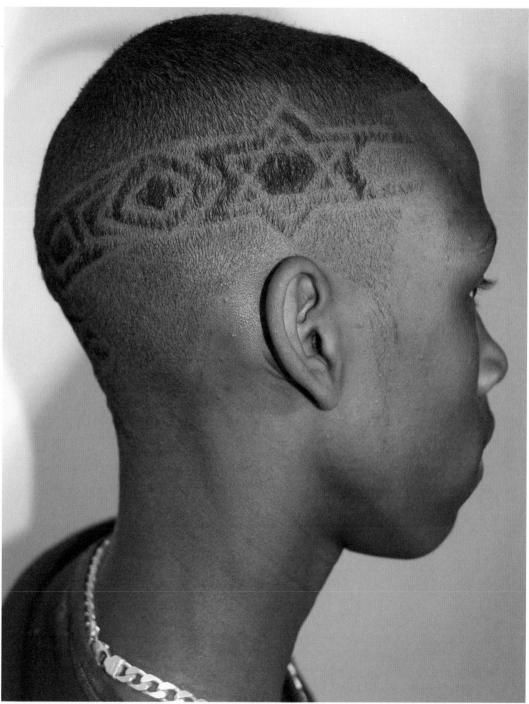

LEFT Hyphy culture, California, 2006 ABOVE Hip hop style, London, 2005

NORTHERN
SOUL

In the mid-1970s a peculiar but fervent movement of soul music worship was taking place in the UK, as young people travelled hundreds of miles to dance all night in the ballrooms and clubs of northern towns to the beat of soul. It became a form of religion as they made the pilgrimage every weekend – bunking trains to get to soul clubs across the country, swapping records at the buffet bar in Crewe Station while waiting for the 1 a.m. train to Wigan and dealing in car parks for the speed that would keep them going at legendary all-nighters.

In its early days northern soul was a subculture created by young people, out of the reach of the media and record companies, bringing colour and passion at a time of power cuts, industrial unrest and football violence. Every Saturday night, around two thousand young people flocked to clubs like Wigan Casino to dance to obscure American soul music from 2 to 8 a.m. The casino was an assault on the senses. Soaring music swept the crowd up in a euphoric frenzy and it smelled of cigarettes, sweat, damp, Brut aftershave and shoes.

Outside the licensing laws, with no alcohol being served, amphetamines fuelled their energetic dance moves which incorporated spins, backflips and moves inspired by Soul Train and Bruce Lee kung-fu films. 'At key points in the track, the whole dance floor would clap their hands in time to a certain pivotal drumbeat and the crack reverberated around the room like gunfire,' remembered journalist Stuart Maconie.

Northern soul was an evolution of sixties mod culture. By 1966, mods in London had either turned to LSD and psychedelia or merged into skinheads, but northern mods still held onto their scooters, soul music and speed. Northern soul combined British style with a love of American music, but it was also a culture of nostalgia – it was the soul music of the 1960s that they

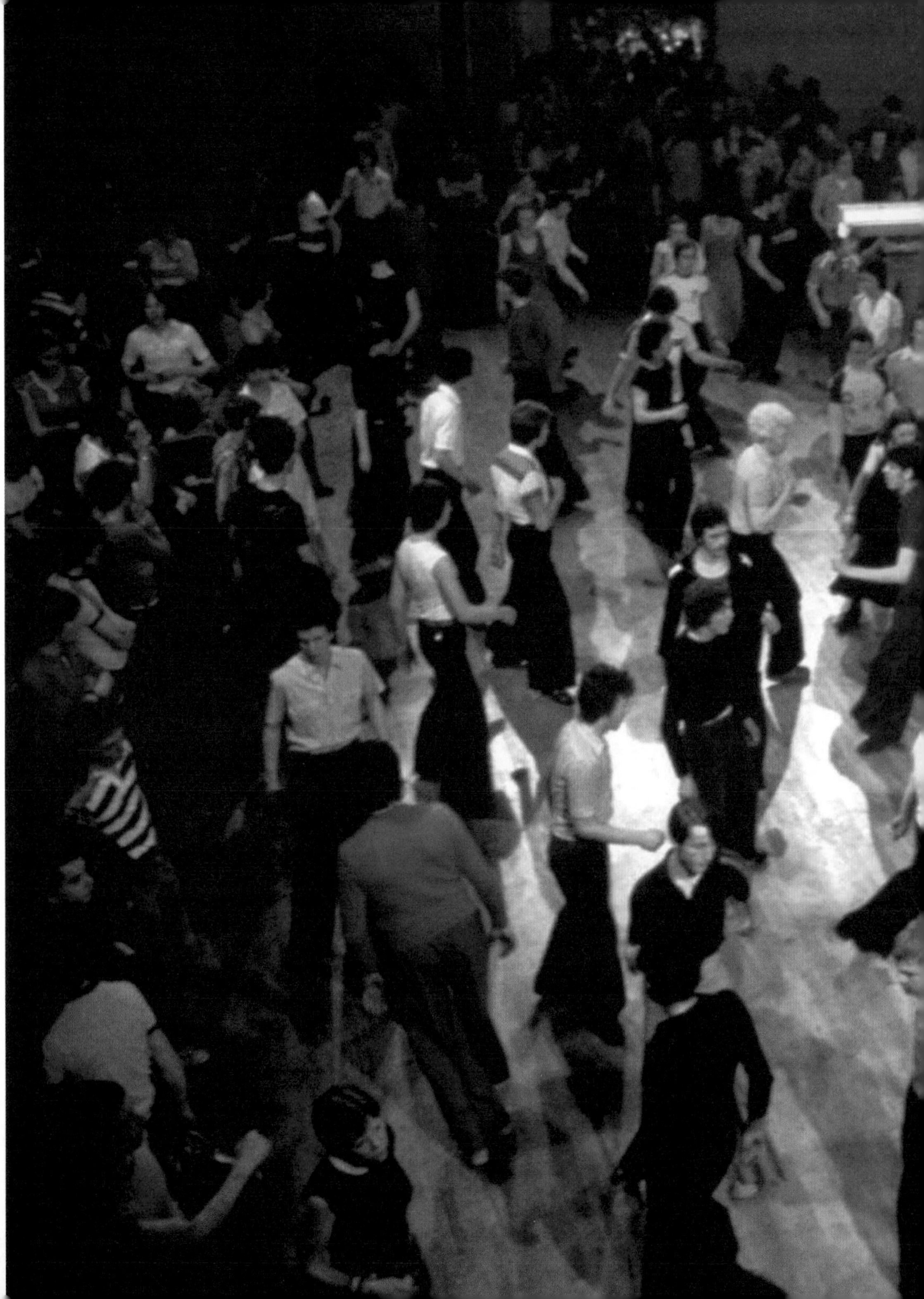

A northern soul fan's customised sports bag, 1975

obsessed over. Their passion was a raw and rougher version of Motown, with hard-to-find recordings and demos from unknown musicians from America. It was first given the name by DJ Dave Godin in 1968 to distinguish it from the uptown soul music scene.

In Manchester, the Twisted Wheel was one of the hottest underground clubs, where DJ Roger Eagle gained a reputation for playing the best soul records. It was originally the Left Wing coffee house, but by 1963 it attracted Manchester mods who parked their scooters outside and gathered in the cramped space to listen to American rhythm and blues and guest performers including John Lee Hooker and Memphis Slim.

The atmosphere was palpable as the crowd, brought together by drugs, would slam-clap to the beat, reverberating from the low ceilings and brick walls. It was a scene for the obsessive and they were dressed in the most up-to-date trends of the day – stylish suits with Brutus shirts and two-tone tonic trousers, or Levi jeans and Fred Perry shirts, their hair grown fashionably longer.

Following police concern around drug misuse and thefts from chemists, the Twisted Wheel was closed down in January 1971. Soul fans searched out new all-nighters across the Midlands and the North – clubs including the Torch in Stoke-on-Trent, the Catacombs in Wolverhampton and the

Blackpool Mecca. When Wigan Casino held a new all-nighter in autumn 1973, no one could foresee what a phenomenon it would become; running for eight years and coming to represent the entire northern soul scene.

1974 saw record attendance at Wigan Casino, reaching its capacity of around two thousand, all in their wardrobe of leather trenchcoats, wide jeans and sports tops. They carried Adidas and Lonsdale hold-alls with a change of clothing to combat the sweat and talcum powder for sprinkling on the dancefloor to make it easier to perform their moves. They sewed badges with the logo of their favourite club on to their bags and vests, the Twisted Wheel's Lancashire Rose symbol or patches with the slogan 'Keep the Faith'. By the end of the 1970s the dedicated soul fans thought badges on vests were passé – it had, by then, been covered too much in the media.

In contrast to the camp 1970s fashions of Slade and Marc Bolan, northern soul style was cool and sharp, a reflection of the early mod style, but durable and flexible enough to offer freedom of movement for dancing. They had jackets with multiple buttons and pockets, fitted vests, Fred Perry shirts, Adidas sportswear, wide-flared trousers and brogues to allow them to show off the dance moves.

Many items of clothing were bought from markets. A soul boy, Chris Brick, remembered: 'It might be a satin jacket with an ice-cream cone on the back. The pants I wore, if I bought them off the peg, were Sterling Cooper. I wore long raincoats, long leather coats. I wore Skinner jeans from Liverpool; sheepskin coats.'

Girls' clothes were similarly functional – they'd travel in wedges or heels and carry a pair of flat brogues or granny shoes for dancing. They wore printed, fitted shirts with a penny-round collar and a tank top and skirts which evolved from A-lines into long, full shapes that swung as they danced.

Yvonne Duckett, costume designer for 2014 film *Northern Soul*, remembered the fashions from the scene in 1974: 'Skirts became full circle and ankle length, with a high waistband or a bib, usually worn with a vest. You had to keep cool – dancing all night, you would get very hot and sweaty. Hair could be short and cropped or pageboy style, and the few black girls on the scene would have short afros . . . we would make clothes together, as you could not buy the look in the shops and we had little money. You felt you belonged to something special.'

In a precursor to rave culture, DJs became heroes, not only seamlessly playing records without gaps between, but acting as promoters to bring acts over from America, often giving forgotten 1960s soul acts a second chance. Anthems included Frank Wilson's 'Do I Love You (Indeed I Do)' from 1965, with only two original copies in existence, and Paul Anka's 'I Can't Help Loving You', a flop on its initial release in 1966 but given new life by the northern soul scene.

1967
Psychedelia in London

Wigan Casino
all-nighters

1968 •

1973 NORTHERN SOUL

1981 •

Twisted Wheel soul nights

Wigan Casino closes

RIGHT Northern soul night at Wigan Casino, 1975

Record stalls were set up at these all-nighters and they traded 7-inch records by favoured labels Staxx, Atlantic and Motown, often at extortionate prices as the records had only been pressed in small numbers. Soul fans immersed themselves in the culture of black communities in America – finding an affinity with their struggles, as well as being drawn to the exoticism that was so far from their way of life.

Dave Nowell in his book *Too Darn Soulful* described the excitement in making the journey to Wigan Casino, 'the knot to the stomach that began with packing your hold-all full of clothes earlier that evening . . . arriving at Charnock Road services, just a few miles down the road from Wigan, was the start of the final high.' It was here that soul fans from all over the country, who had formed tight friendships with one another, would gather an hour before arriving at the casino. They would get changed in the toilets of the service station, putting on their cool jeans and t-shirts.

When Granada TV filmed at Wigan Casino in 1977 for their TV series *This England* which reached an audience of 20 million, the underground scene entered the mainstream. In 1978 it was named by *Billboard* magazine as the world's best discotheque. Dave Withers, a Wigan Casino regular and record collector, spoke of his love for it in the documentary. 'If Wigan shut down . . . there was no next week, I wouldn't know what to do. Instant nostalgia. That would be it. You'd think, "God, I'm going to be looking back for the rest of my life."'

Wigan Casino shut its doors in 1981 but northern soul never disappeared completely. It was revived by northern soul nights across the country, and in Duffy's 'Mercy' video, enthusiastic dancers recreate the mood and atmosphere of a night at the casino.

DISCO

It was the little signs, a piece of glitter in the hair perhaps, which indicated a work colleague in Manhattan's financial district had been at Studio 54 the night before. New York's nightclub scene exploded in the late 1970s, built on euphoric beats, glamour, beauty and a Las Vegas glitz aesthetic, and where drug-taking and sex in the corner of the club became de rigueur.

Disco came at a time of great social change, when hippie ideals had been replaced with apathy and the Vietnam War and the Watergate scandal had deflated hopeful utopian dreams. The fun of disco was pushing the extremes, from clothing to behaviour that reflected social change. It was time for dressing up again, replacing psychedelic folky hippie fashions with shimmering gowns that would compete with the lighting and glitter balls. White dresses glowed under the strobes, capturing each dance move in a fashion photostrip, and lycra and tight jeans were perfect for the streamlined, athletic look that became popular throughout the seventies.

Thanks to the sexual revolution, women dressed how they wanted, going for revealing hot pants and cat suits, some even stripping off their tops completely or kicking off their shoes in an act left over from the hippie era, and taking at their own risk the broken champagne flutes on the dancefloor. Donna Summer was queen of disco, a former gospel singer in a halo of shimmering, glittering gowns and big hair, whose orgasmic epic 'Love to Love You Baby', produced by Giorgio Moroder, was a ground-breaking seventeen minutes long. It was women who would come to represent the disco era, with their soaring vocals and anthemic songs of survival for the repressed or marginalised.

Disco began as an underground movement in the black and Hispanic gay community in 1970s Manhattan, when crime-ridden New York was a dangerous city to be in at night. The feel-good sound served as an effective celebration of gay rights after the 1969 Stonewall riots, sparked by a New York bylaw criminalising two or more men dancing together.

At the end of the sixties, organised crime had moved into former jet-set hangouts, while police cracked down on places violating liquor laws. The city had opened up to the sex industry, with gay bathhouses, swingers' bars and prostitution on street corners. Juice bars were unlicensed and open all night, and became the place for licentious behaviour.

David Mancuso opened the Loft in 1970 in his own Lower East Side apartment, and, considered the birthplace of disco, it broke down social barriers with an authentic gay culture of different races and classes. Mancuso played what would become the disco soundtrack – blues and funky rock, fused with Latin beats and world music, turning into a hot, sexy new sound that spread a message of togetherness and love. The disco beat was said to be close to the rhythm of the heart.

Several clubs went 'gay' to attract a new marketable clientele, creating an early 1970s disco underground with a thriving gay black and Hispanic community. Quaaludes, acid and cocaine flowed freely at clubs like the Gallery, Sanctuary and Salvation, encouraging a newly liberated, carnal atmosphere.

The disco scene sparked competiveness in terms of beauty standards. Now that gay men no longer had to be secretive for fear of prosecution, they could achieve a sculpted body and a definitive style, from angelic all-white clothing, to Hell's Angels leather.

In Bill Brewster and Frank Broughton's book *Last Night a DJ Saved My Life*, these clubs are described as creating a 'clone' gay look: 'Moustaches, lumberjack shirts, jeans and belts – a newly liberated culture creating a super masculine visual code that was defiantly obvious to those in the know.'

In 1976 *New York* magazine published journalist Nik Cohn's 'Tribal Rites of a Saturday Night', which would become the basis for the film *Saturday Night Fever*, recounting the new disco generation in Brooklyn who knocked back tequila sunrises and peacocked in their finest threads. Vincent, the basis for the character Tony Manero, was 'the ultimate Face' at Odyssey disco. While Cohn later confessed he had made up the character of Vincent, basing him on a Sheperd's Bush mod, his story reflected the importance of the new 'dressing up' of disco, where an Odyssey face 'need only be Italian, between the ages of eighteen and twenty-one, with a minimum stock of six floral shirts, four pairs of tight trousers, two pairs of Gucci-style loafers, two pairs of platforms, either a pendant or a ring, and one item in gold.'

TV show *Soul Train* also had an impact on disco coming into the mainstream. It was where America tuned in to see the latest in African American music

ABOVE LEFT The Three Degrees, 1974 ABOVE RIGHT Roller disco, late 1970s

and fashion, and the Soul Train dancers wearing flares, afros and other items that would be connected to disco style.

It was 1977, the year when Studio 54 opened and *Saturday Night Fever* was released, that disco went stratospheric. Studio 54 transformed a derelict theatre into a carnivalesque ampitheatre with ever-changing themes and sets, and vowing to keep out the 'bridge and tunnel' types of the film. It was a spectacular heaven and hell, as famous faces like Brooke Shields, Elizabeth Taylor and Liza Minnelli would briefly come into view through the strobe lights and smoke, and for one New Year's Eve party four tonnes of glitter created a four-inch layer across the dance floor, as if 'standing on stardust'. In 1977 the *New York Times* reported that the 'in' style of dancing was to 'freeze into an exaggerated pose for 20 to 30 seconds, and then continue on normally – until the urge comes to freeze again.'

Co-founder Steve Rubell wanted the Studio 54 clientele to be a 'tossed salad', and his notorious velvet rope was described by Andy Warhol as 'a dictatorship at the door and a democracy inside'. Hundreds queued in the hope of being allowed in; Grace Jones arrived naked so many times that it became boring, while a man in black tie was found dead in an air vent, having become trapped after trying to sneak inside.

The waiters and busboys were bare-chested, in sneakers and gym shorts, and guests were a mix of rich uptown tuxedos, drag queens, Amazonian models and street kids from the Bronx. Bianca Jagger, who could sense a photo opportunity when she saw one, climbed on to a white horse that had been brought into the club for her birthday party, organised by the fashion designer Halston.

For women, disco opened up the dancefloor, creating a safe space to dance. Hasse Persson,

LEFT Studio 54, New York, 1979 ABOVE Disco sandals from Davids, 1979

Stonewall riots
1969

1970
David Mancuso
hosts The Loft

1974

Diane von Furstenberg's
wrap dress

Donna Summer's
'Love to Love You Baby'

DISCO

1975

Studio 54 opens
1977

1979
Death to disco protests

RIGHT Grand Ballroom Opening, 1973

a photographer who recorded the era, said: 'What was interesting is that women felt secure enough to dance nude in the place. This is after the feminist movement of the 1970s: if a woman wanted to be nude that was her privilege, no one would ever touch her or say anything. They were like queens on the dancefloor.'

Hot pants were the perfect disco item, first brought to the catwalk in late 1970 by Yves Saint Laurent and Valentino, and worn on their own or under a slit skirt. Diane von Furstenberg's wrap dress was one of the hottest items of the 1970s, selling more than five million by 1976. Wrapping around the body like a kimono or a body-skimming robe, they could be worn from the office straight to the disco, and suited the sleek, feline look that was in vogue. Von Furstenberg later told a journalist in the 1980s, 'well, if you're trying to slip out without waking a sleeping man, zips are a nightmare.'

Halston's halter-neck jersey dress was one of the most popular of disco dresses for its comfort and ease of wear, as adaptability in fashion became desirable, thanks to disco. In 1979 the *New York Times* reported that women had little time for clothes unless they were comfortable and functional, and 'which can emerge dripping from the pool, shake dry and be used with a skirt for disco dancing.'

By the end of 1978 disco had become a $4-billion industry, with 10,000 discotheques across America and the majority of charting records being disco hits. Even artists like Dolly Parton and Frank Sinatra were taking on the sound, and with this fast food consumption, there would inevitably be a backlash. It culminated in 1979 with rock fans destroying 100,000 disco records at a baseball game in Comiskey Park, Chicago in 1979.

PUNK

In the summer of 1976 a youth movement fuelled by contempt swept through Britain, returning rock music to its origins – with the purpose of shocking the establishment. On the King's Road young punk fans wore their school blazers covered in razor blades, safety pins and even condoms. Chains were swiped from the toilets of the Roxy club to be used as fashion accessories, and the Sex Pistols, along with Vivienne Westwood and Malcolm McLaren, became dangerous enemies of the nation's morals. It was a cross-pollination of fashion, graphic art and music, culminating in a take-over of the Queen's Silver Jubilee with the indelible image of Elizabeth II punked up with a safety pin through her nose. Four years later punks had become as iconic as beefeaters and the red telephone box, featuring on postcards and gathering around London's Piccadilly where they could charge tourists for photos of them in their out-there dress and acid-coloured mohawks.

Punk is considered to have two different origins – in New York around 1974 in the Bowery clubs of CBGB and OMFUG, and in London in 1975 at Malcolm McLaren and Vivienne Westwood's King's Road boutique. Punk in New York was an artistic rebellion where the clothing was black and ripped, a dirtied rock'n'roll look, while in England punk had a political message. It was a rebellion against the establishment through outrageous slogan t-shirts, bondage wear and anything that was ripped up and uglified, making a statement in the face of unemployment, service strikes and poverty.

Punk was about DIY fashion, buying from thrift stores, fixing with a safety pin, deconstructing fabrics, tearing up pieces of tartan, old combat fatigues and suit jackets to create something new. Even a black bin bag could make a style statement. 'That was a perfect, perfect item of clothing. You'd just cut out a hole for your head and your arms and put a belt on and you looked stunning,' said Sex Pistol Johnny Rotten.

New York in the early 1970s had lost its sense of optimism; the hippie dream had died, and there was a punk rock movement growing from the dank east village clubs. Their clothing reflected nostalgia for rock'n'roll, with black leathers and jeans inspired by Marlon Brando and the Fonz, but their t-shirts were ripped, their clothing was held together with safety pins and they wore sneakers rather than motorcycle boots. Musician Richard Hell had the ultimate rebellious haircut – an exaggerated schoolboy cut, as if he had taken a razor blade to it. 'A guy with a haircut like that couldn't have an office job. And no barber could even conceive of it. It was something you had to do yourself,' he said.

As the Ramones and other New York punk bands were inspired by the rockers, so were the early incarnations of Malcolm McLaren and Vivienne Westwood's fashion empire. In 1971, they took over the lease of a shop at 430 King's Road and rebranded it Let It Rock, selling Teddy boy jackets, customised with coloured velvet collars. McLaren was a follower of Situationism, a movement which encouraged 'happenings', such as his plan for setting alight Madame Tussaud's waxworks of the Beatles. His favourite Situationist slogans, such as 'You're going to wake up one morning and know which side of the bed you've been lying on!' were emblazoned on t-shirts along with images of pornographic pin-up girls, creating a bricolage from retro imagery with slogans.

It was in April 1973 that the New York and London movement collided, when Westwood and McLaren went to New York to display their designs and ended up at the Chelsea Hotel with Andy Warhol, the New York Dolls and Richard Hell, who was a source of fascination for McLaren, describing him as 'deconstructed, torn down, looking like he'd crawled out of a drain hole.' McLaren brought the look back to London, and inspired by the New York Dolls, decided to create a pop group who could showcase the fashions of the shop. They changed their look from Teddy boy style to rocker, calling the shop Too Fast to Live, Too Young to Die. They sold sleeveless black t-shirts, customised with studs spelling out 'scum' or 'Venus', zips placed over each nipple and bleached chicken bones linked with chains that spelled 'rock'.

In 1975 they again rebranded the shop as SEX, with a sign spelling it out in big, pink, rubbery letters. Their clothes sold to a relatively small clique of young London clubbers and rubber fetishists, although Westwood's t-shirts, costing £15, were out of range for most of the kids in the shop. 'Punk fashions are a load of bollocks. Real punks nick all their gear from junk shops,' Johnny Rotten would say.

Soo Catwoman and Debbie Juvenile were regulars in the shop, while Chrissie Hynde and punk girl Jordan were outrageous sales assistants. 'She was amazing,' said Westwood of Jordan. 'I had been distressing clothes, thinking others would follow suit, but no one did till Jordan [started] ripping her tights, and later Johnny Rotten.'

In the summer of 1975 McLaren selected a group of misfits to form his anti-band, the Sex Pistols. 'Creating something called the Sex Pistols was my painting, my sculpture, my little artful dodgers,' he said. Amongst them was John Lydon, called Johnny Rotten because of his teeth, who was spotted outside SEX with safety pinned trousers and a Pink Floyd t-shirt with 'I hate' scrawled on it. Steve Jones, in the infamous Bill Grundy interview, wore a Vivienne Westwood t-shirt with a pair of breasts printed at chest height.

Sid Vicious wore the Ramones style of black leather jacket and studded belts on his jeans, ripped and held together by safety pins, with toilet roll around his neck as a tie. Westwood credited Sid for first using safety pins: 'A mate who owed him money ripped up his apartment one night – shredded the rug, the walls, his clothes, everything. He had to use the pins to hold his trousers together.'

The New York Dolls inspired Westwood and McLaren's most controversial motif – the swastika,

ABOVE Punk couple, London, 1980 RIGHT London punks, 1979

1971
Let it Rock opens
on the King's Road

1975

PUNK

1977

Queen's jubilee

Sex Pistols form

Zandra Rhodes
Conceptual Chic

1979
Sid Vicious dies

TOP LEFT Poster for the Sex Pistols' single 'God Save The Queen' BOTTOM LEFT Punks, London, 1983

combined with skulls and crossbones. They didn't wear the swastika in support of Hitler, but to shock. Siouxsie Sioux, known for her swastika armband, said, 'It was an anti-mums and dads thing. We hated older people always harping on about Hitler, "We showed him" and that smug pride. It was a way of watching someone like that go completely red faced.'

In 1976 the shop was restyled yet again, as Seditionaries, to reflect the angry political mood. Westwood put the 'A' for Anarchy sign on the labels of their clothing. The straight-jacket inspired trousers, 'bondage kecks', became 'a declaration of war against the consumerist fashions of the high street', according to McLaren. Similarly, the Royal Stewart tartan was the preferred punk fabric for its contradiction as a royal fabric as well as that of the Jacobite uprising.

The punk look spread quickly during Britain's heatwave of 1976 and into the next summer, when the anarchy flag spread worldwide as the international press gathered in London for jubilee celebrations and the royal pageant. The anthem of that summer, the Sex Pistol's 'God Save the Queen', echoed out across the city and played from a barge

occupied by the punk contingent. At gigs punk fans pogo danced, described by *Rolling Stone* in 1977 as 'jumping up and down and flailing one's arms around. It is as far as one can get from the Hustle, and it is the only way one can dance if one is wearing bondage pants tied together at the knees.' It was invented by Sid Vicious, who said: 'I didn't know how to dance, so I just jumped up and down and bashed people.'

Punk style would evolve into t-shirts, black leather studded jackets, bondage trousers, skinny jeans, Doc Martens, Mohawks and body piercings, with an exaggerated uglification from 1979 onwards. It also became incorporated into haute couture – from Zandra Rhodes 'Conceptual Chic' collection, with punk hardware of chains, zips and safety pins inspired by the look at the Roxy club, to Versace's safety-pin dress, famously worn by Liz Hurley in 1994, and the designs of Alexander McQueen.

But, as John Lydon said: 'At heart, punk was a street culture. It came from kids on the street, doing it yourself. The trouble is that punk got co-opted, and distorted by the media. People find it hard to get away from the clichés, from the popularised eighties version of punk, and it became a stereotype.'

LEFT & ABOVE London punks in the mid-1980s

NEW ROMANTIC

London's Soho in 1978 had yet to be populated by stylish bars and boutiques, instead it was a place of seedy strip clubs and lurid signs, with the odd espresso bar on Old Compton Street. But every Tuesday night, in a basement club called Billy's, an exotic, outré crowd of Central Saint Martins College art students, former punks and soul fans gathered for a Bowie night, run by singer and club host Steve Strange and DJ Rusty Egan.

Billy's was formerly the Gargoyle club, where, in the 1920s, Noël Coward, Evelyn Waugh and Tallulah Bankhead would meet. Now a new set of bohemians and wannabe revolutionaries congregated to escape from the dirge of unemployment and piles of rotten bin bags on the pavements following the strikes throughout the 1970s. Drawn by the flyer announcing 'Fame, Fame, Fame – jump aboard the night train,' this group of eccentrically dressed peacocks were elitist, vain and obsessed with glamour, and it was exactly what London needed at this time of economic discontent. The new romantics appeared at a turning point in British history – in 1979 when Thatcher was elected, and into the 1980s, which brought on the greed is good ethos, yuppies and power dressing.

In February 1979 the club night moved to the Blitz in Covent Garden, a 1940s wartime themed wine bar. Steve Strange, dressed as Pierrot or in his Gestapo leather coat with a silver-topped cane, controlled the door, with swarms of hopefuls queuing to gain entry. It was Eurocentric, with a playlist of continental electronica, including Kraftwerk and Giorgo Moroder. They liked to think their club nights replicated the Weimar era Berlin of *Cabaret* and *The Blue Angel*, where a decadent, hedonistic nightlife defied the economic upheaval. 'From the foppish fashions of the video boom to the repetitive beats

of house and techno, the whole of the Eighties was prefigured in the bitchy brew of Blitz,' wrote Dave Rimmer in his book on the new romantics.

Those who got in to the hottest underground club were dressed as futuristic teds with winklepickers, quiffs and false eyelashes, as gangsters or Robin Hoods with whitened faces and frilled collars. It was where pirate met military hero, eighteenth-century fop or French revolutionary whore. Costumes came from charity shops, adapted and customised on sewing machines with enthusiasm by young, hungry fashion students: a Jacobite swathed in tartan, a jacket covered with Malteser wrappers, a necklace made from gilded seashells. 'The kids that turned up faithfully every week at his Blitz club were dreamers,' said former Blitz Kid Iain R. Webb. 'We wanted to be fashion designers, pop singers, writers, photographers, makeup artists and film-makers. We wanted to impress Steve, not least to get through the door, but also because we knew he was one of us. He didn't care that you weren't a famous celebrity, he loved that people made an effort – and we did, for him.'

The up-and-coming crowd included milliner Stephen Jones, DJ Jeremy Healey, singer Sade, Karen Woodward from Bananarama and Boy George, who worked on the cloakroom alongside model and club DJ Princess Julia, where he would alternately dress as a punk geisha, Boudica or Carmen Miranda, trying to outdo the others. Musician Gary Kemp bought a white, swashbuckling blouse from a Saint Martins art student who wrote his name in the label – it was an as yet unknown John Galliano.

Kemp's band, Spandau Ballet, inspired by the foppish electro new wave scene at the Blitz, stepped in to create the type of music they were listening to in the club. Their 'secret' gigs in the arthouse Scala cinema and on the derelict HMS *Belfast* created hype, becoming the hottest tickets in town for faces like Siouxsie Sioux, Billy Idol, and members of Ultravox and Japan, and every record company clambered to sign them. The media quickly caught on to the headline-making antics of the controversial cross-dressing and exhibitionism, and journalists would gather outside the club in the hope of gaining access to the clubbers who had called themselves 'the cult with no name' or 'the movement'. But it was a double-page spread in *Sounds* magazine in September 1980 that would give the movement a name that would stay with them – the new romantics, referencing the new wave and the cult of Romantic poets like Lord Byron and Percy Bysshe Shelley.

At the Blitz club, Mick Jagger was famously refused entry by 'door whore' Steve Strange because they were over capacity. But David Bowie, whose song 'Heroes' was the anthem of the club, was granted admission when he turned up one night to cast for his 'Ashes to Ashes' video, filming the next day on a pebble beach in Hastings with Strange and a select group of Blitz kids. In an interview with the *NME* in 1980 David Bowie recalled the 'grim determination' of the scene. 'I was taken to one extraordinary place by . . . Steve Strange? God, what was it called? Everybody was in Victorian clothes. I suppose they were part of the new new wave or the permanent wave or whatever.'

Many of the new romantics got their clothes from Covent Garden shop PX, where Steve Strange worked as a shop assistant. It was a pre-club meeting place for the clubs regulars, who would dress in the collection of angular jackets, bellhop and Cossack outfits. *The Times* reported that the 'new romantic look is anything but threatening. It is jolly, extravagant and must be a light-hearted relief for the jeans and sweatshirt generation who have had precious little chance to dress up . . . because romance has a far wider appeal than punk could ever have, it is going to be big. The biggest thing, say the fashion people, since the mini skirt and the sixties. What the peasant skirt did for seventies fashion, pirates will do for the eighties.'

Eventually the movement became a victim of its own success, and with too many people clambering to get into the club and queuing round the corner, Blitz was closed in October 1980, just as Spandau Ballet and Steve Strange's band Visage released their first singles – 'To Cut a Long Story Short' and 'Fade to Grey'.

Strange opened up a new club, Club for Heroes, and at the same time Vivienne Westwood was sewing 'Clothes for Heroes' on to the label of her latest collection. Following on from punk's Seditionaries, Malcolm McLaren had advised Westwood that her next fashion look 'should be romantic.' Westwood was drawn to the paintings of the Incroyables and Merveilleuses of the French Revolution, combined

TOP RIGHT Blitz kids, Rainbow Theatre, London, 1980 BOTTOM RIGHT Boy George
and a friend watch Spandau Ballet perform on HMS *Belfast*, 1980

with swashbuckling pirates. They were clothes for those who dared to bring attention to themselves. Malcolm McLaren's new band Bow Wow Wow, with their lead singer Annabella Lwin discovered by him in a launderette, became the models for this pirate collection.

Westwood later recalled: 'The first collection was a combination of inspiration from Geronimo to pirates. It was a combination of those things, along with the French Revolution with all its promise of change, and its violence and sexiness. It's a look that has gone all over the place, reached into theatre and film. You can see it in *Pirates of the Caribbean*, even: Jack Sparrow could have been on the Pirates catwalk.'

The new romantic subculture was short-lived, over by 1981, but its legacy was a chart dominance of new wave synth-pop bands like Human League, Soft Cell, Duran Duran and Bananarama. The flouncing shirts and dramatic, androgynous dress most associated with new romantics would soon be launched on the high street, even finding its place in the wardrobe of Lady Diana with a feathered hat or frilled neckline. It changed the focus of style in Britain in the 1980s to glamour, high fashion and a sense of improvisation, where coloured eyeshadow and lipstick could be common wear for men.

GOTH

Goth culture was a dark and macabre offshoot of the original punk movement, capturing at its heart the theatricality of Victoriana and the occult. In the late 1970s, encouraged by Siouxsie Sioux's DIY fashion, it fused the symbols of Gothic literature and film with glam, punk and the new romantics, creating a distinctive style of its own.

Gothic fashion developed its own language, inspired by nineteenth-century Gothic stories by Ann Radcliffe and Horace Walpole, Mary Shelley's *Frankenstein*, gothic horror films, and medieval and Victorian rituals, creating a form of beauty from death and the dark side of life. Goth is considered more than just a subculture – it's a state of mind that references an obsession with darkness, from the Eye of Ra symbol, used on the Sisters of Mercy *Vision Thing* album cover, to the pagan pentacle and the crucifix. While edgy and extreme, there's a misconception that goths are devil worshippers and Satanists, when in fact it is romance that lies at the heart of it.

'It remains a visual shortcut through which young persons of a certain damp emotional climate can broadcast to the other members of their tribe who they are. Goth is a look that simultaneously expresses and cures its own sense of alienation,' writes Valerie Steele in *Gothic: Dark Glamour*.

While the Victorian era is often depicted as repressed and prudish, it was also a time of eroticism and elicit behaviour, as reflected in Gothic literature, with opium dens and sexual deviance. It was the costume of the Victorians that would inspire modern goth dress, particularly with the cult of mourning, where a widow would wear black for a year. These mourning gowns were supposed to be plain, with a veil to hide the grief, but women added fashionable touches like plunging necklines, sequins and off the shoulder sleeves. The goth predisposition for jewellery incorporating skulls, clasped hands and Celtic imagery came from the centuries-old custom of charms and amulets for memorials and to ward off death. Further inspiration for the twentieth-century goth can be traced to the 1920s silent movie vamp as portrayed by Theda Bara, Bela Lugosi's *Dracula*, and the shadowy, jagged style of German Expressionist film which explored the horror, darkness and fragility of the mind.

The first wave of British post punk bands – Bauhaus, Siouxsie and the Banshees and the Cure – mixed a fetish look of punk and glam rock, twisted into a dark, horror style. David Bowie referred to his 1974 album *Diamond Dogs* as gothic in its styling and five years later, in 1979, Joy Division's manager, Martin Hannett, described their sound as gothic – the musical equivalent of *Nosferatu*. Bauhaus created the blueprint for gothic music, with their 1979 hit single 'Bela Lugosi's Dead', which used glam vampire imagery. But Siouxsie Sioux was the originator of what became known as the goth look, with her black back-combed hair, red lips and white skin, and she would continue to be the influential fashion icon for goth culture.

In 1980 Steve Strange, following the cult success and then mainstream adoption of the Blitz club fashion, started a club called Hell, on Henrietta Street in Covent Garden, one of the first goth clubs. Strange would lead his guests out through the backdoor to the graveyard of St Paul's Church. Against this sacred backdrop they would take acid and hallucinate, reflecting the gothic fascination of fear within the mind. In 1982 the Batcave club opened in London, with its motto 'blasphemy, lechery and blood', run by a group called Specimen. It attracted media attention for the macabre and experimental stylings of the clientele and a Bowie-esque fluidity of sexuality, following the outré punk and new romantic style.

Through the 1980s goth found international popularity with the music and style of the Cure and Sisters of Mercy. It worked as a dark antithesis to the sugary pastels and pale denims of 1980s mainstream fashion with male and female goths wearing dark eyeliner, black nail polish, occult jewellery and borrowing from the Edwardians, Victorians and punk. Goth also overlapped with rock culture with the wearing of band t-shirts, and the indie and crusty scene with tattoos, piercings and combat trousers. Later, goths would dye their hair red, purple or bleached blonde.

Doc Martens were the favoured footwear of goths, just like punks and skinheads before them. But any black boots would do, buckled, heeled or with a pointed toe. A black coat was worn to be bulky and encasing and goth girls had laddered tights or fishnets, an easy and accessible way of dressing. In cities like London and San Francisco goth fashion suited the young and poor – it could be bought in thrift stores, and if tights had a hole in them, they could be ripped further into cobwebs. A writer for the *New York Times* recalled that in San Francisco the Haight-Ashbury crowd 'turned as abruptly and completely black as if a wall of ink had crept up from the Pacific and saturated everything, save for occasional outcroppings of little silver skulls.'

There was a moment in the 1980s when goth music was the dominant sound, the Cure was one

PREVIOUS PAGE Singer Siouxsie Sioux, London, 1980 ABOVE Goth weekend, Whitby, 1990s

of the biggest bands in the world and Cher wore her outrageous spiderweb gown to the Oscars, but it was a subculture that had kept relatively under the radar, eclipsed by hip hop and house music.

Gothic culture was given a new lease in the 1990s, with the release of film adaptations of Bram Stoker's *Dracula* and Ann Rice's *Interview with a Vampire*. They inspired a new goth look for men, with long hair, frilled shirts and heavy coats; a replication of the Victorian dandy, where a pale, thin body was desirable.

Marilyn Manson would further develop goth music and style, creating a dangerous, dark culture surrounding his music, which was played up in the media. In 1998 *Melody Maker* announced that goth was back: 'The shadows are stretching, darkness is encroaching and with it comes a mutated form of the human race. They dress differently, they talk differently and they group together in secret, hidden haunts.'

A number of tragic events in the late 1990s and 2000s propelled goth culture into the headlines. Following the Columbine High School shootings goths became the folk devils – depressed and dangerous teenagers hanging on to the words of Marilyn Manson. Towns in America even set up outreach units to combat goth culture. The popularity of girl witches in the media, such as in the television

LEFT Goths in Trafalgar Square, London, 1987 ABOVE 1980s goth girl, Camden market, London

Siouxsie Sioux and the Banshees
1978

1982

Batcave club
opens

GOTH

1994
*Interview with a
Vampire* in cinemas

Marilyn Manson
Antichrist Superstar
1996

2001
Alexander McQueen
gothic-inspired designs

LEFT Goth girl, Whitby, 2015

show *Charmed* and film *The Craft*, was matched by a surge of interest in Wicca, reportedly the fastest growing religion in twenty-first-century America. But goths, while individualists and outsiders, are overwhelmingly peace-loving, with an interest in fantasy and mysticism, and generally misunderstood in tabloid press.

The gothic girl, while edgy and dark, has always been depicted as alternative, cool and mysterious and she knows her own mind. In this way, goth characters like Winona Ryder as Lydia in *Beetlejuice* and Lisbeth Salandar in Stieg Larsson's *Millenium* series have become feminist icons – outsiders who are intelligent and think for themselves.

While punk was quick to become mainstream, goth took twenty years to be integrated into high-street fashion, filtering down from fashion designers like Alexander McQueen, who used erotic, macabre imagery in their designs. McQueen created goth experimentations, with the skull design for his scarves and leather corsets stitched like the scars of Frankenstein. His often avant-garde designs would be adapted for the high street, with crossbone bracelets and Victorian-style blouses. Alexander Wang's Autumn/Winter 2015 Walk On the Darkside collection, was 'goth for Instagram', devoid of colour and tapping into a style of industrial, street goth.

The cyber goth, inspired by films like *The Matrix* and *Blade*, also references the look of Fritz Lang's 1927 film *Metropolis*, which presents the belief that the human race will become obsolete due to technology. Custom-made cyberwear, from PVC and rubber, often with the appearance of an oil slick, are like custom-made pieces of art. The industrial goth wears leather, black denim and vinyl, paired with a t-shirt of their favourite industrial metal band, and has the hardwear of the punk – spiked jewellery, black leather, metal rings and chains.

Goth fashion thrives in Europe, in Germany in particular, where large annual festivals are held. The M'Era Luna festival in Hildesheim is the biggest goth gathering in the world along with Whitby Goth Weekend in England, where goths from all over the world gather to celebrate the lifestyle.

LEFT & ABOVE Whitby Goth Weekend 1980s; 2014

ACID HOUSE

Britain in the late 1980s had become cocooned and cold, wrapped in the selfish 'me' generation of Margaret Thatcher's government. But out of this yuppie society, the smiley face rose up as a beacon of hedonism and unity as 1988 became the new Summer of Love.

Acid house wasn't created from one core influence, instead it was the convergence of numerous scenes and movements, including the hedonism of disco, the DJ innovations of early 1970s hip hop, the German futuristic electronica of Kraftwerk, the inclusive pilled-up attitude of northern soul, the hippie Ibiza scene and Chicago and Detroit house and techno. This mash-up was reflected in rave style – a combination of hippie psychedelic clothing, comfortable club gear and football casual sportswear.

House music in the 1980s emerged from Chicago's gay and multi-racial club the Warehouse, and was given the name as a way of describing the type of music on Warehouse DJ Frankie Knuckle's playlist – classic disco, Euro synth pop and soul. The Warehouse was a massive sweaty pit of predominantly gay and black partygoers, so hot that they ripped their shirts off, echoing the hardcore trend for men going shirtless in British clubs. At the same time a group of Euro-electrophiles in Detroit, including Kevin Saunderson and Derrick May, were creating an industrial techno sound which would be imported into the clubs of Europe.

Manchester in 1986 was coming into its own as a centre for alternative music and pop culture. The Hacienda's legendary Nude night, where Mike Pickering played the latest Chicago sounds, drew in a regular crowd of pleasure seekers, or 'scallies', like the Happy Mondays, while in-house dancers would demonstrate jacking, a house music dance style that originated in Chicago. 'The wardrobe was trainers and t-shirts; the night even saw the first appearance of the ubiquitous flares,' wrote Peter Hook of the band New Order. The Hacienda was different from other clubs as the door policy was reversed. 'In those days what I call "thugs in ties" could get in by wearing the shittiest of clothes, as long as they weren't trainers,' Tony Wilson once said. 'But if you turned up in a beautiful Armani top, or even Fred Perry with great Gazelles on, they'd go, "You're not coming in." We reversed that completely, so immediately for the "Perrys" . . . it was the first place they had to go to.' The club scene exploded in 1987, with the introduction of the drug ecstasy (MDMA). It was, as Sean Ryder remembered, 'When life suddenly went from black and white to Technicolor.'

In Ibiza, the after-hours open-air club Amnesia was attracting a bohemian crowd as DJ Alfredo Fiorito mixed Kate Bush and U2 with Chicago house, sending euphoric waves through the loved-up crowd dancing under the stars and continuing after the sun had risen.

In summer 1987 DJs Paul Oakenfold, Danny Rampling and Nicky Holloway visited Ibiza and took ecstasy for the first time, falling in love with the Balearic vibe at Amnesia. They came back to Britain with ideas for starting up Ibiza-like clubs in London, where the scene was more about posing at the bar of trendy West End nightspots. Danny Rampling's Shoom started as invite only but word spread and just weeks later hundreds of people were waiting outside the club, trying to get inside the strawberry-smoke filled space where they were swept up in a loved-up ecstasy embrace. Normal life was dull compared to this blissful hedonism on offer and regulars gave up their jobs to devote themselves to the experience, supporting themselves by making t-shirts or music.

The Ibiza group developed their own fashions, which was a mix of hippie, beachcomber and casual. Their baggy trousers, t-shirts, dungarees, paisley bandanas and Converse trainers were comfortable and fit for dancing until drenched with sweat, rather than posing at the bar. There were Aztec or flower designs, batik print hoodies, and a new age influence that suited the Balearic vibes. Inspired by Shoom, shops like Sign of the Times in Kensington Market stocked rave gear, mixtapes and fanzines dedicated to the scene.

In 1988 Q Magazine reported that outside Heaven nightclub in central London were 'hundreds upon hundreds of garishly dressed persons looking like nothing so much as a disembarking planeload of Gatwick holidaymakers,' while inside, 'the chanting, partying, grinning inmates are gleefully bouncing their way through some unique and untutored choreography.' The Trip at the Astoria, in the heart of London's West End, was pure acid house. When the crowds poured out of the club at closing time, they would continue dancing in the street to the sound of sirens and traffic, crying 'acieed!'

Shoom created t-shirts with the yellow smiley face logo, and it became the defining emblem of acid house. The smiley had originally been designed in 1963 by American advertiser Harvey Ball for an insurance company to motivate their workers, and it then appeared on stickers at free festivals during the psychedelic movement. But it took on a whole new meaning as the face of acid house, featuring on album covers, badges and flyers, and in fashion design.

PREVIOUS PAGE Acid house ravers, 1989 ABOVE Synergy, London, 1988

With its link to the hippies, 1988 was dubbed the Second Summer of Love, as many began to embrace New Age ideas, such as eco-activism, paganism and anti-capitalism, while there were reports of a decrease in football violence as casuals hugged it out with their rivals instead of fighting. Boy's Own were a group of football fans, including Terry Farley and Andy Weatherall, who had been into the London soul scene before embracing the Balearic sound. They penned their own fanzine aimed at 'the boy (or girl) who one day stands on the terraces, the next day stands in a sweaty club.' In spring 1988 Boy's Own declared: 'Ethnic print gear is in and the B.A.F movement have taken over the city centre. What does B.A.F stand for? "Baggy As Fuck!" That's wot. Everything's gone baggy – bananas, shirts, kecks,

even happy haircuts, the lot.' The baggy scene exploded in Manchester in 1989. Suddenly everyone looked like Shaggy from Scooby-Doo in acid-bright colours, over-sized hooded tops, long-sleeved shirts, flares, cricket hats and Converse.

Rave would begin to develop its own codes and accessories influenced by the effects of ecstasy. Sucking on dummies and chewing gum alleviated teeth grinding, while the strong scent from Vicks Vaporub intensified ecstasy's euphoric effects. 'Hold it down!' and 'all right, mate?' were rave buzzwords, and strangers hugged one another, had a sip of their water, and shook hands in a sincere ecstatic state. Gas masks caught on as ravewear when rave duo Altern-8 brought chemical warfare suits to their performances.

ABOVE Clubbers at the Astoria, London, 1988 RIGHT The Hacienda, Manchester, 1989

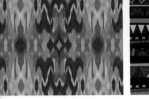

1990
Kate Moss on the cover of *The Face*

1994
Criminal Justice Bill

Ecstasy in Britain
Manchester's baggy scene

1980
1987
ACID HOUSE
1989

Frankie Knuckles at
the Warehouse
The Second
Summer of Love

RIGHT Ravers at the Hacienda, Manchester, 1989

With acid house's increased popularity, the original Balearics were unhappy when their favourite clubs were flooded by gurning teenagers, dubbed 'acid teds', who would take off their shirts and tie them around their waists.

One of the first outdoor dance events was the August 1988 Boy's Own party in a barn near Guildford. 1989 would see an explosion in warehouse parties and outdoor events and over the next few years parties would be held in fields in Hampshire, abandoned mills and industrial estates in Lancashire, turning into a game of cat and mouse between the police and the ravers. The Castlemorton Common festival became the biggest illegal rave in history as crusties and weekend ravers partied for seven days, leading to front page outrage and the introduction of the Criminal Justice and Public Order Act of 1994, giving police power to shut down gatherings.

The *Sun* newspaper had been on board with the acid house scene at first, describing it as 'cool and groovy' and offering smiley t-shirts for sale. But a few weeks later, it changed tack to warn of the dangers. Acid house was now, according to the *Sun*, a 'hellish nightmare engulfing thousands of youngsters'. Topshop even banned the sale of smiley t-shirts on the back of negative press.

Despite the outrage, house music was a pervading force in the early years of the 1990s. 'The horrible truth is we are living in a country where the only real prospect many people have of a decent future is to retreat into wonderland,' *The Face* magazine asserted in 1993. Escaping into wonderland had become big business by the mid-1990s with superclubs like Ministry of Sound and Cream, superstar DJs with crossover hits and Ibiza attracting half a million young people each year to its famous club scene.

GOA
TRANCE

Goa, as a former Portuguese colony, had been on the hippie trail since the 1960s for its more relaxed way of life than in other parts of India. It would become a psychedelic trance drug-and-dance paradise, attracting rave tourists from around the world who found they could live well on a few dollars a day.

The scene became linked to a phosphorescent, neo-hippie traveller and raver look of dreadlocks, rainbow coloured tie-dye tops and fisherman's pants, bought cheaply at one of the many stalls by the beaches. The music, which would morph into psychedelic trance, incorporated cinematic, natural sounds and a build-up to a sense of euphoria.

American-born Goa Gil was the instigator of what would become the Goa trance sound. He arrived in India in 1970, at the age of eighteen, one of the original freaks along with Yertward Mazamanian, known as Eight Finger Eddie, founder of the famous Anjuna flea market in 1975, who would look after the draft-dodgers and addicts who arrived there. Gil fully embraced India's philosophy by living with yogis in the Himalayas and spending time in Goa. 'When I first went to Goa there was only one house with foreigners on Anjuna,' he recalled. 'It was Eight Finger Eddie's house, and maybe twenty of us freaks were staying there with him. The first parties were campfires on the beach where we were playing guitars, drums, flutes, and the full moon parties all grew out of that. Later on we got some electric equipment, started making jam sessions and then bands, and then it went on to full DJ parties with techno music in the early 1980s. We pretty much initiated the whole way of life that Goa came to be.'

In the 1980s Gil began playing eurobeat and hi-NRG for open-air parties at the Northern Goan beaches of Anjuna, Little Vagator and Big Vagator, which would be more associated with acid consumption than MDMA. Speaking to *DJ* magazine, Goa Gil spoke of dance as 'an active meditation', and the scene would merge different spiritualities of Taoism, Hinduism, Zen Buddhism and

PREVIOUS PAGE Poi performer, Anjuna, Goa, 1999 LEFT, CLOCKWISE FROM TOP Hippie commune in India, 1971; revellers at a New Year party at Vagator, Goa, 2000

GOA TRANCE · 171

Mayan beliefs, with an appreciation of hatha yoga and New Age philosophies.

This 1980s hippie party scene on Goa, with its white beaches and tropical forests, was spread by word of mouth, and began attracting backpackers and New Age travellers from around the world. By the early 1990s the scene flourished at the Bamboo Forest and Disco Valley, and was then brought back to Britain, Israel, Sweden and Germany. Committed revellers would travel to Goa for the party season during winter in Europe and then search out similar places, like Ibiza, during the summer.

Bali, Nepal and Thailand were backdrops to a rave scene which thrived in environments where living was cheap, with readily available drugs and where the traveller garb of ethnic prints and native, hand-crafted jewellery tied around necks and wrists was easy to get hold of. Despite dressing as if they had no money, this backpacker scene was often criticised as a middle-class way of breaking from social confines without the need to work. They would take themselves away from the comforts of the west – to hammocks on beaches, squat toilets and long distance bus journeys – all in the name of adventure.

In the UK at the beginning of the 1990s ravers were drawn to free festivals and parties instead of high-priced clubs. After the Criminal Justice Act in 1994, places like Goa and Thailand would provide the utopian ideal of free parties, away from the confines of government regulation. Goa trance would fill the yearning for those lost free parties and the loved-up glory days of acid house.

Goa's trance parties made use of ultraviolet light with fluorescent decor, clothes and body paint. Ultraviolet lamps, as opposed to lasers or strobes, could easily be brought into a forest environment. This fluorescent and phosphorescent décor incorporated glowing, New Age patterns, images of fireflies and mushrooms, aliens and Hindu goddesses – anything that was vaguely spiritual. Goa trance developed a fashion for sixties hippie items of tie-dye, flares, ethnic batik print, sarongs, shell necklaces and Hindu bindis sold in packets at markets.

Goa became a popular destination for young Israelis when they were permitted to travel there after 1988, often looking for a refuge from the pressures of home life after two years in National Service. With a traditional conservative dress in Israel, an ethnic, hippie fashion was being sold in boutiques in Tel Aviv in the 1970s, a look which would become known as 'shanti' style, and which fitted with life on a kibbutz or travelling in India. Simon Reynolds in Energy Flash described the male trance look as the '"Jesus Christ Superstar/ Khao San Road in Bangkok" backpacker look (straggly-bearded, lank-haired, body odour optional) and the "Israeli hunk/ Milli Vanilli" look (mocha skin, long mane of oily curls, hairy muscled chest on display).' The female trancer was a mix of hippie chick and beach babe, with halter tops, long skirts and hair tied back from the face. The handkerchief tied around the head came from

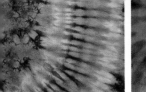

1968
Hippies arrive in Goa

1975
Anjuna market
founded

1988
Israelis travel to India

GOA
TRANCE

1993
Return to the Source
party in London

Goa trance reaches peak
1996

the Israeli influence, described by Reynolds as like 'kibbutz women picking oranges'. A psytrance style of dancing was nicknamed 'the Israeli stomp'.

Unwilling to let go of the scene when they returned home, they held parties at beaches or in forests, replicating the mystical settings of Goa parties. *i-D* magazine described trance parties in Tel Aviv, where 'the spirit of Goa is being invoked. Multi-coloured hangings depicting Indian deities adorn the walls. A small side room serves fragrant, nutmeg-infused chai tea. And people talk as well as dance, about recent trips to Asia and recent trips.'

In 1993 club organisers Return to the Source held a party in London, trying to replicate the Goa experience. Due to its popularity, Paul Oakenfold's Perfecto label picked up on the scene. In 1995 labels like Flying Rhino and Dragonfly, and Goa trance parties held across the country, led *i-D* magazine to question if Goa trance was the new acid house. 'Goa's legendary party scene has turned a global network of travellers on to its unique sound. Spiritual, psychedelic and blowing up across the world.'

Psytrance clubs would recreate the Goa party feel with fluorescent decorations hanging from the ceilings, ultraviolet light and chill-out rooms that offered massage, tarot card readings and market stalls selling t-shirts, jewellery and bindis brought back from Goa. Space Tribe created t-shirts and clothing with swirling, brightly coloured fluorescent prints with tie-dye and optical illusion effects – a form of alien hippie chic. Travellers brought their backpacker style home with them, with men unshaven, with long hair, and women sporting nose rings, fimo bracelets and dreadlocks. Their skin and hair glowed under the fluorescent light as paint and hair dye were also applied. In New York, promoters Tsunami held psytrance parties, and as the *New York Times* reported in 1998, 'the walls and ceilings are covered with gaudy streamers, papier-mache sculptures of magic mushrooms, butterfly mobiles and retina-scorching mandala tapestries.'

ABOVE LEFT Gogo girl dancing at final frontier, 1990s ABOVE RIGHT Trance night, Rimini, 1990s

Psytrance's superclub incarnation was Gatecrasher in Sheffield. Psytrance offered an escape from reality, particularly in a world changed by the 2001 attack on the World Trade Centre in New York. Followers of the scene took psychedelic drugs, many of which were legal, like magic mushrooms and Salvia. The hippie focus of Goa trance also fed into a neo-bohemian fashion trend in the late 1990s, as seen with Madonna's incarnation as earth mother and kabbalah and yoga devotee.

In 2004, the *Guardian* reported: 'The music has electronic, tribal and thumping layers that can almost instill a meditative state in the clubber . . . originating from peace-loving travellers, it carries the philosophies of peace and free thinking. But now it has moved from the circles who adore yoga and meditation to a mainstream crowd.' As Goa became more popular, travellers, or 'trancepackers', would search out the next Goa that had yet to be discovered by the crowds. The scene had all but died out in Goa with a police crackdown on outdoor parties due to noise and drugs issues. One of the new places was the jungles of Puerto Rico, where in 2000, El Cuco, a three-day psychedelic trance festival, took place.

GRUNGE

When Marc Jacobs sent supermodels down the catwalk wearing grunge haute couture in 1992, it seemed like the pinnacle of mainstream integration for a slacker youth culture from the Pacific Northwest. Grunge was everywhere that year; flannel shirts and ripped jeans in Urban Outfitters, Cameron Crowe's film *Singles* in the cinemas, and young Hollywood icons Johnny Depp, Winona Ryder and Drew Barrymore dressing down as if to say they had better things to worry about than fashion. But critics wondered if Jacobs had missed the point. When he sent Kurt Cobain and Courtney Love pieces from his Perry Ellis collection, she revealed that they set them alight. 'We were punkers – we didn't like that kind of thing,' she said.

Before Starbucks, Microsoft and Kurt Cobain, Washington in the 1980s was a sleepy backwater of lumberjacks and blue-collar workers with a DIY music scene centred around shopping malls and video stores, dance parties in garages and gigs in alleys. Musician Jeff Gilbert said: 'Seattle isn't a glamorous town at all. It was pretty pathetic. Very depressing, that's where the music came out of.'

Seattle-based indie record label Sub Pop began signing up local acts like Mudhoney and Nirvana, promoting a dirty punk rock sound for alternative radio and music festivals like Lollapalooza. This Seattle sound began to be championed in the UK by radio DJ John Peel and by the music press. The bands had names that suggested something beautiful but twisted, in contrast to their earthy style of dress. Alice in Chains was an imagining of a bondage *Alice in Wonderland*, Soundgarden was named after a sound sculpture on a beach near Seattle, and Pearl Jam came up with a story that their name was inspired by lead singer Eddie Vedder's grandmother, Pearl, who would make hallucinogenic jam.

Grunge was the antithesis of 1980s greed. Generation X were the slackers depicted in Douglas Copeland's 1991 novel of the same name. They raged

PREVIOUS PAGE Grunge style, London, 1992 RIGHT, CLOCKWISE FROM TOP Musicians hang out in a cafe in Seattle; Nirvana fans attend a vigil for Kurt Cobain, 1994; Seattle street style, 1993

against corporate America and consumerism, and as Winona Ryder said in the film *Reality Bites*, 'they wonder why those of us in our twenties refuse to work an eighty-hour week just so we can afford to buy their BMWs. Why we aren't interested in the counterculture as if we did not see them disavow their revolution for a pair of running shoes.'

Grunge fashion was born from necessity and practicality, and rejected the aesthetics of conventional beauty. It threw together borrowed items, thrift store lumberjack shirts and cheap finds from the bottom of a bargain bin. In Washington they wore flannel shirts, jeans and long johns as cheap, utilitarian clothing for keeping warm in the rainy state. Pearl Jam's Jeff Ament said, 'It was partly function and partly what was laying around.' Musicians on the punk rock music scene looked like loggers or steel workers with their denim jackets and unwashed look that was quite different from the flamboyant heavy-metal style popular at the time. Up on stage in sweaty Seattle music venues they became sex symbols, with their long, unkempt hair covering their eyes or sticking to their faces with perspiration, heavy socks worn with work boots and flannel shirts tied around the waist. Soundgarden's Chris Cornell layered his shorts over long johns, a style worn by skateboarders, while Kurt Cobain, self-conscious of his small size, bulked himself up with layer upon layer of flannel and denim. His most recognisable items, a green jumper and pair of

patched jeans, were borrowed from close friend Lori Barbero from the band Babes in Toyland. 'His coat got stolen one night and I gave him that sweater that he wore all the time, a greenish, brownish v-neck,' she said. 'It had thumb holes because I'd been doing that since I was a kid.'

Grunge also celebrated the idea of the reject, the nerd who doesn't fit in, particularly with the ironic 'Loser' t-shirts by Sub Pop which came to represent grunge's unlikely heroes like Cobain, who was regularly picked on at school. The groundbreaking music video for Nirvana's 'Smells like Teen Spirit' was faded, brown and dirty and with porn-star cheerleaders wearing t-shirts bearing the anarchy symbol. In summer 1991 the song was circulating around Seattle and by autumn that year it was everywhere. By Christmas, their album *Nevermind* had sold two million copies, an extraordinary success for an alternative band from a region most famous at the time as the real-life setting for surreal television show *Twin Peaks*.

Music industry insiders from Los Angeles and San Francisco descended on Seattle to find the next Nirvana, along with the world's media, all covering the hot story of the year. The clubs in Seattle swarmed with grunge tourists hoping to catch sight of newly famous bands or glimpse Drew Barrymore, who was dating Eric Erlandson from the band Hole. Kurt Cobain and Courtney Love became fascinating cartoon characters for their rock'n'roll antics and

Courtney Love and Kurt Cobain, 1992

drug abuse. A *Vanity Fair* interview with Courtney in August 1992 caused shockwaves when she casually revealed she had been doing heroin while pregnant. With high profile users, heroin was seen to be chic, cool and on MTV. It wasn't just the grunge girls – models were getting high, and photographer Corinne Day created photospreads which came to represent the idea of 'heroin chic'.

When *The Face* magazine visited Seattle to see the scene for themselves, they found 'clean-cut Keanus and Winonas who sport variations on grunge rock national dress: cut-off army fatigues, sometimes with long johns; hiking or combat boots; the occasional nose ring and the obligatory flannel shirt worn around the waist.' Seattle clothing store Linda's Tavern

became a haven for grunge kids when it was revealed it was where Kurt Cobain bought his hair dye. Owner Linda Derschang said, 'In a way "grunge fashion" was a non-fashion. That's why it was so funny that it turned into a Marc Jacobs line for Perry Ellis.'

This anti-fashion street style was given its own spread in American *Vogue* in December 1992, entitled 'Grunge and Glory'. It showcased the high-fashion version of alternative youth culture, with plaid shirts, work boots and floral dresses, with prices far out of reach for a kid on minimum wage. It wasn't long before it spread to the world of haute couture. It tied in to a new look for models when a waifish girl from Croydon was signed as the face of Calvin Klein and would became the model representation of grunge,

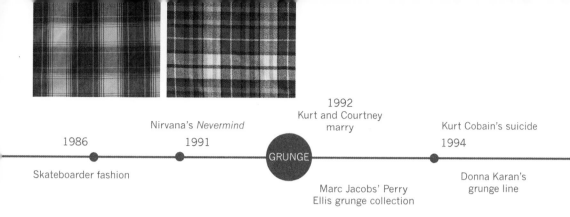

1986
Skateboarder fashion

Nirvana's *Nevermind*
1991

GRUNGE

1992
Kurt and Courtney
marry

Marc Jacobs' Perry
Ellis grunge collection

Kurt Cobain's suicide
1994

Donna Karan's
grunge line

especially when on the arm of Johnny Depp. Klein had seen Corinne Day's photos of Kate Moss in *The Face*, her imperfect teeth on display as she laughed and played on a beach. It was completely natural, youthful and so different from the Amazonian supermodels with their all-American tanned limbs, glossy smiles and blow-dried hair.

Marc Jacobs developed a mood board of his new obsessions – black and white photos of Kate, images of Nirvana and Pearl Jam – and it was this that inspired his new collection for Perry Ellis. Jacobs sourced cheap flannel shirts and sent them to Italy to be made in expensive silk, and charity shop wool caps were remade in cashmere. James Truman, editor of *Details* magazine, said: 'Grunge is about not making a statement, which is why it's crazy for it to become a fashion statement . . . Buying grunge from Seventh Avenue is ludicrous.'

Donna Karan created a grunge look in 1993 with Fair Isle knits, long skirts, baggy jackets and big brown socks. *The Face* magazine covered these new fashion lines, praising Anna Sui's rainbow grunge and Mark Jacobs' hippie version, but criticising 'the establishment' of Klein, Karan and Ralph Lauren. 'For those sitting in gilt chairs, who'd never come across the Subpoppers and cohorts, it was time to wake up and smell the coffee.'

Kurt Cobain died in April 1994 and modish Brit Pop was already waiting to step into grunge's tired place and take centre stage. Grunge would be revived twenty years later as hipsters went environmental and railed against consumerism, mimicking a faux anti-fashion stance with ripped denims, floral dresses and big boots worn at festivals, by fashion bloggers and on the catwalk.

RIOT GRRRL

'All girls to the front!' went Kathleen Hanna's cry from the stage, encouraging the girls in the audience to push through into the mosh pit, typically a crushing and aggressive male space. Girls formed tight groups and made their way to the front, holding hands as a unified force, spurred on by Hanna screaming out 'Rebel Girl', as she did back kicks and jumped around on stage. Hanna of Bikini Kill was the inspiration for many a teenage girl in the early 1990s as her band called for a 'revolution girl-style, now'.

Along with punk bands like Bratmobile and Heavens to Betsy, Bikini Kill led a new grassroots movement in the early 1990s called riot grrrl, offering a feminist voice amongst the male-dominated music scene. An 'angry girl' mood was in the air, and they shared their ideas through writing, art and music, reigniting the feminist movement fifteen years on.

Olympia, Washington had a thriving punk scene with a DIY feel of creating and recycling, and like many women on college campuses in the early 1990s, girls were interested in the ideas of feminism. They created artworks and photographs with feminist messages as a reaction against reports of violence against women and sexism in the media. They put together fanzines like *Jigsaw* and *Girl Germs*, by Allison Wolfe and Molly Neuman, who would form the band Bratmobile. Guitarist Tobi Vail chose the name Bikini Kill for their band as it juxtaposed sex with violence, and along with Bratmobile, named the movement riot grrrl after their zine.

The bands drifted to Washington D.C. for its progressive punk and political scene, and over the summer of 1991 would hold their first riot grrrl conference and regular meetings at a punk activist commune. At their gigs, riot grrrls handed out zines, photocopied pamphlets with impassioned pleas against rape, domestic violence and the everyday harassment of women. They were provoked

PREVIOUS PAGE Bikini Kill and Joan Jett, 1994 LEFT L7's Donita Sparks ABOVE Lollapalooza festival, 1993

by the way women were depicted in the media, from Miss America to the *Sports Illustrated* swimsuit issue, where women were treated as objects rather than as humans with something to say.

They encouraged girls across the country to take the name riot grrrl and create their own message. Zines like *Adventures in Menstruating* dealt with issues such as eating disorders, child abuse and harassment. *Hungry Girl* wrote: 'SLUT. Yeah, I'm a slut. My body belongs to me. I sleep with who I want . . . I'm not your property.'

Rock for Choice was a rock concert which took place on the eve of a pro-choice march in D.C. in April 1992, the biggest protest Washington had seen since the Vietnam War. Riot grrrls wrote pro-choice messages on their skin, and drew hearts and stars on their arms and stomachs, revealed by a rolled up t-shirt or knotted shirt. Riot grrrl meetings were also being held across the country and in Olympia a *LA Weekly* journalist recounted that 'most were dressed in traditional Olympia girl style: short-cropped dyed hair; rumpled vintage dresses; bright Woolworth's lipstick.' While the dress was a Generation X grunge style of boots and floral dresses, riot grrrls also subverted girlish wear of tartan skirts, baby doll dresses and knee high socks with piercings, converse trainers and tattoos.

They turned conventional ideas of femininity on the head by dressing provocatively, or created spectacle through image using a schoolgirl look.

They were girls who had grown up with Madonna as a controversial icon, who used sex to empower and wore underwear as outwear. Camille Paglia said that Madonna 'dresses like a whore, but she always knows what she wants. These girls are dressed to kill but ready to fight.'

Kathleen Hanna ripped off her t-shirt mid-performance, and in her bra and skirt, revealed to the audience the word 'slut' written on her stomach. It was a confrontational move to demonstrate the contradiction of an audience wanting to see a woman performing in a bra, yet at the same time considering her a slut if she did so. She would wear tongue-in-cheek outfits – a dress printed with a speedo-clad man, bra tops, school shoes and socks. 'I was trying to do interesting gender stuff,' Kathleen said, 'Like, fucking with the idea that I'm a woman who still has what's considered masculine traits.'

While feminists like Andrea Dworkin were vocally anti-porn, Kathleen worked as a stripper, and believed it could be a free and powerful choice. 'Being a stripper is what let me be in Bikini Kill,' she said in the documentary *The Punk Singer*. 'Do I wish that there was a job that paid me that amount of money and gave me that flexibility and that I didn't have to take my clothes off? Sure, but it didn't exist . . . I worked at McDonalds and I was a vegetarian and I just felt like it was the same thing. I was a feminist and I worked at a strip bar.'

Jennifer Finch from L7 would carry out even more outrageous stunts, such as revealing a naked

ABOVE Riot grrrl zine ABOVE RIGHT Riot grrrl attitude

crotch on live television show *The Word* or pulling her tampon out and flinging it into the audience. Finch told *The Face* in 1992: 'I get concerned about girls now not having the same experience I did with civil rights and feminism. Punk rock is what really got me into playing music because it proved you could really do anything and it didn't matter if you were a girl or a boy.'

Courtney Love was often seen as a kind of riot grrrl leader, but she would more often be an antagonistic force to the cause. Her band, Hole, along with L7 and Babes in Toyland, were lumped with grunge, labelled riot grrrl, or jokingly referred to as foxcore by Sonic Youth's Thurston Moore. Courtney's style – pale skin, red lips, bleached blonde hair with dark roots and a dirty, vintage dress – was labelled the 'kinderwhore' look. She was a disintegrating type of pretty, while singing of being ugly. 'She smiles, a huge red lipsticky grin

. . . wears babydoll dresses, often a size too small, which gives the impression of a grown woman presenting herself as a child,' wrote an interviewer in *The Face* in 1993. Hole's lyrics on their first album, 1991's *Pretty on the Inside*, were an angry, feminist take on abortion, eating disorders and tortured notions of beauty. Like Babes in Toyland's Kat Bjelland, who argued that she had the look first, Courtney accessorised her ripped 1930s dresses with a guitar and smudged make-up. In a profile piece in *Vanity Fair* in 1992, she said: 'It's a good look. It's sexy, but you can sit down and say, "I read Camille Paglia."'

'Culturally we don't allow women to be as free as they would like, because that is frightening. We either shun those women or deem them crazy,' said Kim Gordon in her autobiography, *Girl in a Band*. 'For a girl, cool has a lot to do with androgyny, and after all I played with boys, and also played with

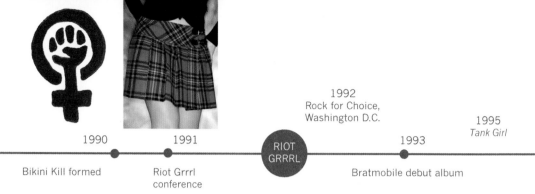

1992
Rock for Choice,
Washington D.C.

1995
Tank Girl

1990

1991

RIOT
GRRRL

1993

Bikini Kill formed

Riot Grrrl
conference

Bratmobile debut album

RIGHT Babes In Toyland at the Dreamland amusement park, 1992

other boy bands. The hardcore scene was extremely male, and in the post-punk American hardcore scene you didn't see many girls onstage.' What girls could do was play up their image, like Kira Roessler of Black Flag, in bra, garter belt and stockings.

Newsweek covered the riot grrrl movement in 1992, calling them possibly 'the first generation of feminists to identify their anger so early and to use it.' They quoted sixteen-year-old Samantha Shapiro, who said 'people compliment me on my combat boots. That something so angry is fashionable for women shows things have changed.' She said she admired Bikini Kill because 'they're being as sexy and as womanly as they can be . . . They're about accepting and appreciating differences – enhancing them.' Like Washington D.C. band Fugazi, who refused to create tour merchandise or speak to the media, riot grrrls put out a media block so they could control the way they were presented, despite huge interest from mainstream outlets in the movement.

While many of the bands had broken up by the mid-1990s, the angry girl message had seeped into the mainstream, with musicians like Tori Amos and Alanis Morissette signed to major labels. *Tank Girl*, a comic book and then film character, was seen as a feminist hero in biker boots, bra and tattoos: '23, sassy, with an imperfectly shaved head and the style of riot grrrl.' 'Girl power', a term first used in a Bikini Kill zine, would become the slogan of the Spice Girls. With a fourth wave of feminism taking place, modern incarnations of riot grrrl can be seen in the band Pussy Riot, Slutwalks and the writings of Caitlin Moran and Lena Dunham.

BRITPOP

Britpop was a fresh neo-mod style that played to British ordinariness – the faux cockney accents of Blur, the Gallagher brothers' Manchester swagger and the lad and ladette culture of drinking pints, wearing vintage Adidas and watching football. It heralded a burst of colour and optimism to counter the influx of American grunge and slacker culture.

Obsessed with nostalgia, Britpop looked to the past with rose-tinted, Union Jack-framed glasses. Bands were influenced by the mod sounds of the Kinks, the Beatles and the Jam, and played up to Swinging Sixties imagery with mod suits and shirts by Burberry and Fred Perry. They wrapped themselves in the flag, just as mods had done in the sixties, but amped up with Noel Gallagher's Union Jack guitar and Geri Halliwell's tiny dress at the 1997 Brit Awards.

Lyrics dealt with typical British subject matters through a comic, cynical realism – drinking cider in the park, coming up on an E in a field in Hampshire, and that first awkward sexual encounter. Pulp's 'Common People', considered the anthem of Britpop, was a song about a rich girl wanting to slum it with a working-class boy.

Damon Albarn, lead singer of Blur, said in 1993: 'If punk was about getting rid of hippies, then I'm getting rid of grunge. It's the same sort of feeling: people should smarten up, be a bit more energetic. They're walking around like hippies again – they're stooped, they've got greasy hair, there's no difference.'

The mid-1990s was a time of optimism in British culture where Kate Moss was a truly British rock'n'roll supermodel, wearing a Union Jack sweater by Clements Ribeiro at London Fashion Week, and British artists Damien Hirst and Tracey Emin shook up the art world. The cream of the Britpop crowd, Moss, Pearl Lowe, Noel Gallagher and Meg Matthews, went for dinner at the Ivy and Caprice, swigged champagne and snorted cocaine at the Met Bar in Mayfair. *Shallow Grave* and *Trainspotting* were cool, homegrown Brit versions of Quentin Tarantino films. The postmodernism of Tarantino's *Pulp Fiction* also appealed to an era of borrowing from the past. Britpop reflected a sense of optimism in politics, going from eighteen years under a Conservative government to New

PREVIOUS PAGE The Flamingo club, London, 1996 ABOVE Pulp pin badges, 1995

Labour coming into power in 1997. Teenagers, who had been born under a Thatcher government, had known only one ruling political party, but the music had the sense of change coming.

The beginning of Britpop can be marked as April 1994, when Blur's album *Parklife* went straight to number one in the charts and a new Manchester band called Oasis performed 'Supersonic' live for the first time on 1990s youth show *The Word*. While illegal rave parties were being hosted in fields and warehouses across Britain, Radio One was still playing over-produced classic rock such as Simply Red, Genesis and Annie Lennox. In 1993 Radio One hired a new controller, Matthew Bannister, to shake up the station and he got rid of the old guard in favour of young, hip DJs like Steve Lamacq, Jo Whiley and

Chris Evans. Soon alternative bands like Pulp, who had been slogging for twelve years, would become the popular choice for teenagers. From keyboardist Candice Boyle's furry bubble-gum-coloured sweaters to Jarvis Cocker's 1970s geography-teacher look of flares with Fair Isle sweaters and fey dance moves, Pulp were alternative, retro and ironic.

Indie band Suede also offered a new British hope with their woozy glam punk songs that spoke of council houses and drug abuse. Lead singer Brett Anderson was thrust onto the April 1993 cover of *Select* magazine with a Union Jack behind him and the headline, 'Yank's Go Home!' Anderson wanted to create a defined world, like the fandom of the Sex Pistols and the Smiths. 'You could dress like them and watch the same films as they watched

ABOVE Brighton, 1998 ABOVE RIGHT Blur's Damon Albarn, 1996

and read the same books and that's what I always wanted to do – to kind of establish a lexicon, almost – and that can obviously drift into self-parody at some point.'

At the same time, Blur were disillusioned by a tour in the United States. Damon Albarn told the *NME*: 'I just started to miss really simple things. I missed people queuing up in shops. I missed people saying "goodnight" on the BBC. I missed having at least fifteen minutes between commercial breaks . . . so I started writing songs which created an English atmosphere.' The first single released from *Parklife* was 'Girls and Boys', reaching number five in the UK charts just weeks before Kurt Cobain would commit suicide. It marked a new celebratory image of the teenager on boozed-up package holidays instead

of being depressed in their bedrooms. Blur stood out from the grunge look of the time, particularly when Albarn wore a sixties mod suit on stage at Glastonbury in 1992.

Oasis swaggered on stage with oversized mod parkas and Paul Weller haircuts. As Liam Gallagher said: 'I'm obsessed with my hair . . . you've got to have a decent haircut if you're the front man of a band.'

High-street fashion would also pick up on the new Britpop trend, copying the mod look with the Duffer of St George Parka and t-shirts with mod slogans and Union Jacks. Ozwald Boateng created a version of the mod suit with bright colours in tweed and wool and Paul Smith celebrated the 1960s dandy, printing his signature multi-colour barcode on to a Mini Cooper.

1996
Vanity Fair declares
'London Swings Again'

Geri's Union Jack dress
1997

1993   1994   BRITPOP

Suede on the
cover of *Select*

Blur's *Parklife*

New Labour
wins election

1995
Blur and Oasis
chart battle

Bands were fronted by gutsy women like Elastica's Justine Frischmann in Fred Perry shirts and Doc Martens, and Louise Wener from Sleeper with her short haircut with bleached sections at the front, a style that Geri from the Spice Girls would take as her own. They demonstrated that teenage girls as well as boys could also idolise female guitar players. Britpop girls wore Converse sneakers, band t-shirts bought from gigs, vest tops over t-shirts and mini skirts like Sonia from Echobelly, and cut their hair into a short graduated crop. Louise Wener remembered when Sleeper played at Brixton Academy: 'There are lines of kids in Sleeper t-shirts, stretched out all the way to the back. At the front are gangs of girls with my haircut, those two skunk blonde stripes in the fringe. Carbon-copy leather jackets. Carbon-copy drainpipe skinny jeans.' Kenickie had a Saturday night alcopop and chip shop glamour, described as 'an earthy, cartoon-glam aesthetic, half old Hollywood starlets, half explosion in Claire's Accessories.' Bassist Emma Jackson said: 'We realised the importance of the visual and from our inception tried to look "glamorous" in our own way. We favoured short skirts, high heels and synthetic fibres – preferably in an animal print, celebrating our idea of glamour.'

In 1996, thirty years after *Time's* piece on Swinging London, *Newsweek* declared London the coolest city on the planet and *Vanity Fair* announced 'London Swings Again', with Patsy Kensit and Liam Gallagher photographed for the cover under a Union Jack bedspread. Ben and Jerry's even created a Cool Britannia flavour of ice cream as Oasis and Blur embarked on a chart battle with their singles 'Roll With It' and 'Country House'. 250,000 people descended on Knebworth to watch Oasis, a moment that Noel Gallagher pronounced as history in the making – their generation's Woodstock.

But if Britpop at first rejected American culture, it soon turned on itself by becoming a parody of what it originally stood for, with the celebration of

Britpop band Kenickie, 1996

laddish culture – Euro '96 football, beer and page three girls in Blur's 'Country House' video. Despite Tony Blair's election victory, with help from Britpop stars, 1997 was considered the end of the scene. Oasis had run out of steam, with their third album not living up to the hype, and Britpop casualties were suffering the effects of drug and alcohol abuse. With the death of Princess Diana at the end of August of that year, it seemed the hope of the last couple of years had faded.

Britpop was looked at as an embarrassment of excess and indulgences – and outdated with its celebration of lad culture. Blur's Graham Coxon described it as 'Austin Powers: bad teeth and horrible suits', but despite the laddish culture, it had brought excitement back to guitar music in the midst of house-music domination, and heralded a dress-down yet glamorous fashion for girls, with trainers and Doc Martens and cool, cropped hair.

EMO

Emo was a movement for a generation raised on the internet, who found escape in music and dressed like young skateboarding goths brought up around suburban shopping malls. They wore band t-shirts, jeans, studded belts, striped tops and piercings, with hair dyed a vivid Manic Panic or Fudge hue and swept forward across the face.

Emo kids were considered thoughtful, intelligent and introspective; punk fans with an appreciation of the tortured lyrics in songs by the Smiths. Rather than the protests and anarchic behaviour of previous subcultures, they kept their emotions internal. Like generations of teenagers before them, they used music to help them understand problems at home or at school. They could close the world out from their bedrooms and exchange messages and music with each other online.

In an article in *i-D* magazine in 2015, emo was described as 'the last real British youth subculture . . . for many people in their twenties, emo doesn't just mean the studded belts, cut-my-wrists-and-black-my-eyes lyrics or black and red aesthetic; it conjures up strong memories of a distinct lifestyle. And there hasn't been a movement as striking and widespread to make its mark on youth culture since.'

Emo culture came into the mainstream by the 2000s, with bands like My Chemical Romance, the Get Up Kids and Fall Out Boy, influenced by the hybrid skater style of American rock bands of the 1990s who wore Vans trainers and hoodies. But its origins can be traced to the hardcore Washington D.C. music scene. Bands like Rites of Spring were labelled emotional hardcore when they sang of something more meaningful than traditional hardcore offerings. Lyrics spoke of feelings of isolation, despair and heartbreak, like the words to 'Remainder': 'Tonight I'm talking to myself, there's no one that I know as well, thoughts collide without a sound, frantic, fighting to be found.' Members of Rites of Spring would form Fugazi, an uncompromising and ethical punk band who refused to sell merchandise or do media interviews.

PREVIOUS PAGE & ABOVE Emo teens, Santiago, Chile, 2007 LEFT Emo boys, Buenos Aires, 2009

In the 1990s, 'After years of raging sameness, hardcore desperately needed a brain; after years of studied, ironic detachment, indie desperately needed a heart. What they found was each other. And what it got called was emo,' wrote Andy Greenwald in *Nothing Feels Good: Punk Rock, Teenagers, and Emo*.

Emo came to represent punky pop with a teenage fan base. Weezer embraced a geek sensibility, with lead singer Rivers Cuomo in the black-rimmed glasses that would become an emo style. Green Day had a California punk and skater look, with hoodies and t-shirts over long-sleeved tops and Billie Joe Armstrong's spikey hair bleached or dyed pink.

Following the September 11 attacks in 2001, the consequent mood of fear and uncertainty, and with the internet picking up speed, emo would fully emerge as a youth culture of technology and introspection around 2003. Emo bands like Jimmy Eat World, My Chemical Romance and Dashboard Confessional broke through, despite, as Andy Greenwald said, that 'being called emo is a scarlet E across your guitar strap'.

One of the cool, fashionable styles of the time was baggy trousers, hoodies and tight vest tops and the new wave of punk skaters wore Converse All-Stars or Vans, plaid trousers or skirts, and ties worn over t-shirts. They accessorised with studded belts and chains, trilbies and lots of eye make-up. The look crossed over into emo fashion, but with skinny, black jeans instead of baggy skater pants, and the addition of leopard print and vibrant colour-popping stripes. Emos expressed themselves with facial piercings and unique hair stylings.

It was a cross-gender style where girls rejected high heels for trainers, and make-up was also used by boys. Gender lines were blurred as boys showed 'unmanly' emotion and vulnerability, wore bruise-like dark eyeliner, pink eyeshadow and black nail polish and chose punky skinny jeans that were originally only available in girls' lines.

In 2002 Avril Lavigne was the new pop star on the block, marketed as a punky skater girl in baggy trousers, the fashionable loose tie around her neck and coloured streaks in her long hair. She was the closest to an emo girl pop star, in her striped socks and stud leather wrist bands, and like some teenage emo followers she was shy and moody in interviews. 'It's hard to determine if she's hiding behind her large black hooded sweatshirt because she's really timid – or because she simply can't be bothered interacting with people she doesn't know. But after a little while, the sweatshirt comes off and she starts to open up. Dressed in a fitted, long-sleeved black t-shirt, jeans, and her ever-present black Converse sneakers,' wrote *Cosmopolitan* in 2005.

Social networking site Myspace was a vital tool to connect with other emos across towns and countries, share music and messages with one another, and where bands could get their break online. It allowed the creation of an online identity, a username that could be anything they wanted it to be, reflecting a favourite band or fantasy character. On message boards they could also shape who they were and express their opinions in a safe place. But it was this secret internet culture which caused alarm, with rumours that emo was promoting a depressed

ABOVE Emo girl with blue hair and matching shades, Helsinki, 2010

suicide culture and that girls wore chunky bracelets to cover the slits on their wrists. In 2008, the *Daily Mail* described emo as 'a sinister teenage craze that romanticises death' and 'a subculture that appears to glamorise self-harm and even suicide.'

Lauren, fifteen, was quoted in *The Times*: 'I would not say I was depressed or over-emotional but I am shy, so it is a way of expressing myself through my clothes and make-up. It upsets me that other teenagers will pick on us for being different. It's like the 1960s mods and rockers – now it's emos and chavs.'

In Britain, Greater Manchester Police added goths, punks, emos and metallers as an 'alternative subculture identity' to their definition of hate crimes. Emos in countries like Russia and Iran have been known to be persecuted for their perceived threat to society. When records by bands like My Chemical Romance and Dashboard Confessional were available in Moscow from 2003, teenagers with dyed hair and dark eye make-up began to meet up and hang around Pushkin Square. Emo kids were seen as so dangerous in encouraging negative thoughts that the state introduced legislation to be able to regulate emo websites and ban the fashion, including hair that 'covers half the face' from schools and government buildings.

A wave of anti-emo feeling swept through Latin countries including Mexico and Brazil, with a prejudice that emo teenagers were homosexual,

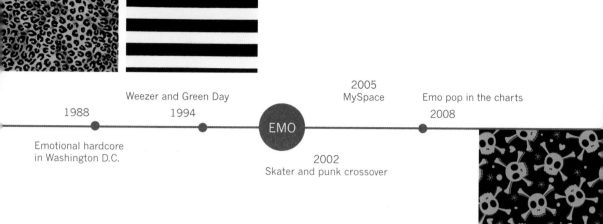

1988
Emotional hardcore
in Washington D.C.

Weezer and Green Day
1994

EMO

2005
MySpace

Emo pop in the charts
2008

2002
Skater and punk crossover

LEFT Scene girl, 2012

anti-social and obsessive. In Chile and Peru there were reports of skinheads
and anarchist punks attacking emo kids for fear of their ambiguous gender
play. But emo culture flourished in areas of urban sprawl and shopping
centres, where they could while away afternoons in record stores and clothes
shops, playing old video games at arcades.

Emo is seen as a particularly teenage scene, with popular bands often
clean-living and eschewing drinks and drugs. The *Twilight* series of books and
films with their rainy setting and lovelorn characters came to be connected
to emo. It would also cross over into the teenage scene subculture, a more
colourful version with cartoon hoodies, fluoro design, bright stripes or tartan
trousers. 'Scene' was originally a derogatory term used for kids who hung
out in skateparks but were more interested in the style and fashion than the
skating, but developed as a poppier version of emo, without so much black.
'Scene people are happy emos,' a scene girl told the *Guardian* in 2010. 'Scene
isn't a fashion thing – we don't like girls that wear tops down to here, but that's
because it isn't good for them. We like loud guitars, we don't like Radio One,
we don't like people who only like music without meaning.'

Emo crossed over into the mainstream without many people even realising
it. By 2010 skinny jeans became the most popular style to wear, skater zip-up
hoodies, studded bracelets and belts were available from Topshop and black
nail polish wasn't just for angst-ridden teenagers.

NEO-ROCKABILLY

Rock'n'roll has experienced a series of revivals since the early 1970s, with its backbeat and country twang a counter-reaction to prog rock and disco, and then to new wave synth sounds of the 1980s.

From the 1990s, neo-rockabillies from Los Angeles to Shanghai looked nostalgically to the sounds of the original trailblazing rock'n'roll hillbilly artists – Elvis Presley, Johnny Cash, Jerry Lee Lewis, Carl Perkins and Eddie Cochran, as well as mixing styles with boogie-woogie and 1960s soul music. It served as a response to modern life and technology, where enthusiasts obsessively recreated the past with vintage clothes and cars.

The fashion became a hyped up movie version of rock'n'roll that incorporated vintage 1940s and 1950s fashions with the punk of the psychobilly movement – black leather, rolled up jeans, white t-shirts, gas station shirts with name badges and arms covered in tattoos.

Women acted out their own pin-up and burlesque fantasies with halter-neck tops to show their body art, homespun gingham or Patsy Kline check, visible bras, and hair dyed black or red and shaped into a Bettie Page style, a beehive, 1940s waves, or with a handkerchief knotted in the hair. 'I go for the whole B-movie thing in a big way – polka dots, prints and loads of colour,' said Irish singer Imelda May, known for her vintage rockabilly look. 'My brother was into rockabilly and he just started me off really . . . he set me listening to Buddy Holly, Eddie Cochran and Billy Fury and that was it – I got myself a blonde quiff.'

It was in the 1970s, after the Vietnam War had changed the lives of America's young population, that the fifties and early sixties were seen as a time of romance and excitement, with sleek cars, fashion and music. It was a time before clean-cut youth lost their shine and swapped quiffs for long counterculture hair. The rock'n'roll era had drive-in movies and diners, high school hops and bobby soxers, and these wonder years were recreated on screen when *American Graffiti* hit cinemas in 1973 and *Happy Days* aired from January 1974, depicting a picture-perfect vision of the 1950s.

From Britain's rainy shores, America had always seemed like the land of opportunity, particularly in the grim 1970s where everything was toned orange and brown. A rock'n'roll comeback concert at Wembley in 1972 with Bill Haley, Little Richard and Chuck Berry was attended by 50,000 people. Teddy boy revivalists wore a more exaggerated, glam rock style; brothel creepers had thicker soles, quiffs were bigger and higher, and drape jackets with bolder velvet collars were rediscovered in jumble sales. Vivienne Westwood's early work recycled Teddy boy suits and rock'n'roll t-shirts with images of risqué pin-ups, which would be sold in her King's Road shop and attracted an early clientele of Shakin' Stevens fans and young punks who took on a bricolage style.

In America punks in the Bowery like the Ramones and the New York Dolls had worn leathers and jeans, but added glam rock touches, in part inspired by the fifties revival that was happening around them. Inevitably punk at CBGB would fuse with rock'n'roll to create psychobilly, distinctive for its electric guitar and upright bass, and what the Cramps in New York in 1975 referred to as 'rockabilly voodoo'.

Teds' fashion by 1977 merged with rockers, where it became standard practice to sport tattoos, wear a simple t-shirt, work boots and jeans, like the motorcycle gangs of the 1940s. As the new style evolved, they became known as rockabillies and referred to themselves as hepcats, with a variety of bands that had the name 'cats' in the title – the Polecats, the Rockats and Stray Cats.

Stray Cats, a young band from Massapequa, Long Island, were the most commercially successful in the UK and USA, starting with their single 'Stray Cat Strut' and their style of tousled pompadour, sleeveless shirts, rolled up jeans and piercings in one ear. They were described by The Times in 1980 as resembling 'the kind of junior hoods who used to patrol the waltzers and funfairs in the days when Peggy Sue was a fresher: extravagant pompadours, Technicolor tattoos and expressions somewhere between a sneer and a pout.' Lead singer Brian Setzer said in an interview in 1981: 'We thought we'd go back to the beginning and do it the way they did it and write new lyrics, write contemporary lyrics. Because high school hops don't really happen anymore. So we write about rock this town, about going into a bar, only hearing disco on the jukebox and getting really mad.'

Los Angeles had a strong rockabilly scene from the 1980s, with rock fans in leather jackets queuing up for the Roxy club or Whisky a Go Go. Rockabilly band the Blasters were one of the most popular in LA by 1981, with their punk background and boogie-woogie piano.

Santa Monica counterculture boutique NaNa further helped shape the neo-rockabilly look and its devoted customers would mix up different styles. The Los Angeles Times described the aesthetic of the NaNa tribe and their 'pastiche of punk staples such as skinny jeans, band t-shirts and brothel creepers, over-dyed military surplus, vintage forties and fifties dresses, mod suits, neon new wave accents, bondage gear and a hint of western twang. Nobody looked alike.' It was a style that the Danish psychobilly band Horrorpops would also promote – Bettie Page and Johnny Cash on acid.

CLOCKWISE FROM TOP LEFT Rockabilly fans, London, 1980s; Mexico City, 2011; Hong Kong, 2013

1975
Psychobilly scene in New York

American Graffiti
1973

Stray Cats
1980

NEO-ROCKABILLY

Amy Winehouse's *Back to Black*
2007

1998
Viva Las Vegas Rockabilly event

LEFT Retro styling in Shoreditch, London, 2007

By the twentieth century bands like Kings of Leon, the Black Keys and the White Stripes brought rock'n'roll back with a stronger country and bluegrass sound. Amy Winehouse, with her love for sixties soul music, channelled rockabilly style, and as her fame rose, so did her look: the beehive got higher, the dresses were tighter and more revealing and her body was covered in more tattoos. A *Rolling Stone* profile in 2007 noted 'her ubiquitous ratty beehive atop a thick mane of dark waves, oversize candy-cane plastic earrings and her black eyeliner drawn into exaggerated Cleopatra swooshes. Her exceptionally thin frame fails to fill out her pencil-straight black jeans, but she wears her black wife-beater nice and snug, and her arms display an assortment of old-school pin-up-girl tattoos, some with their tits hanging out, others – like the one with "Cynthia" inked next to it – in coquettish fifties garb.'

While girls in the 1950s wore poodle skirts and bobby socks, the modern rockabilly woman is more Jayne Mansfield than Sandra Dee – cherry lips and wing eyeliner, bright sundresses, high-waisted shorts, cat-eye sunglasses, animal prints and pencil skirts. It could be the look of a femme fatale in a film noir if it wasn't for those tattoos, celebrated in shows like *LA Ink*.

The *New York Times* described the subculture as 'composed mostly of women, mostly young, who like their cocktails sour, their music with rockabilly twang, and their personal contours on the shapely side . . . more siren than sylph, those women derive a sense of chic, and an unexpected emotional comfort, from reinventing themselves as contemporary incarnations of Ms Page, or as modern-day retro-vixens like Katy Perry or Lana Del Rey, who have elevated the all-American calendar girl to an emblem of hip femininity.'

The rockabilly scene found pockets of enthusiasts around the world, starting with the Great Yarmouth 1979 gathering of British rockabillies and their Yamahas. In Japan, the Thunder Tribe of the 1970s rode motorbikes and wore leather and armbands with the nationalist symbol of the rising sun. A rocker movement continued in the Harajuku district, where they still perform in Yoyogi Park to Jerry Lee Lewis and Elvis with a raised lip and a hip shake. Mexico continues to have a strong rockabilly following with Mexico City band Rebel Cats, along with the Rockalavera weekend festival. The Viva Las Vegas rockabilly event is perhaps the biggest in the world, with its hot rods, fashion displays, tiki drinks and rockabilly bands.

HIPSTER

The modern hipster grew from the gentrified urban areas of Shoreditch in London and Williamsburg in New York, where predominately white middle-class groups of young people who worked in creative industry developed a self-referential, ironic way of dressing and being. While often seen as consumerist – always searching for the hot new thing, particularly with technology – they were environmentally conscious and supportive of independent businesses, with words like 'artisan', 'single origin' and 'craft beer' becoming stereotypical.

Generation Y lived under the shadow of war and terrorism and with this instability and social injustice, they sought comfort in the look of the past and an appreciation of nature, more so after the financial crash in 2008 and increased concerns around global warming. Tweed caps, waistcoats and beards spoke of rural, old-fashioned times. Hipsters wore lumberjack flannel shirts juxtaposed with feminised skinny jeans and King George V beards, like bands Mumford and Sons or Fleet Foxes with their folksy banjo accompaniment. In 2003 *The Hipster Handbook* by Robert Langham described the young people of Williamsburg with their 'mop-top haircuts, swinging retro pocketbooks, talking on cell phones, smoking European cigarettes . . . strutting in platform shoes with a biography of Che Guevara sticking out of their bags.' This description sounds almost modish, but hipsters were more liberal in their thinking and green in their consumerism.

It was the electroclash scene that laid the groundwork for the modern-day hipster, combined with a post-9/11 uncertainty. In 2002 in Williamsburg, Brooklyn, Berliniamsburg was a club for the electroclash scene, where synth groups like Fischerspooner, Tiga, Chicks on Speed and Peaches paid tribute to the 1980s. It was where the idea of Williamsburg as the centre of cool began, and promoter Larry Tee said at the time: 'We try to keep the bridge-and-tunnel people away – except for us the bridge-and-tunnel crowd are from Manhattan.'

PREVIOUS PAGE East London couple, 2014 ABOVE Electroclash band CSS, 2007

Simon Reynolds in his book *Energy Flash* described Berliniamsburg as stepping into a parallel universe, where 'rave never happened'. He noted the new wave and new romantic looks of 'asymmetric haircuts, ruffs, skinny ties worn over collarless t-shirts, punky-looking studded belts and wristbands, little cloth caps. But nobody really looks like they're from 1981 – in fact, they look much sharper and, on the whole, not nearly as silly.'

From electroclash came nu rave, around 2006, where the scene in London favoured bright colours and a merge of different tastes and styles. Skinny jeans became the essential style for boys and girls, a nod to the punk style of Pete Doherty and Kate Moss, and bands like the Klaxons and Bloc Party.

An adaptation of the word 'hipster' has been used since the 1920s, derived from 'hep', to describe someone different and cool. There was the jazz-loving hepcat of the 1940s, the beatniks who hung out in coffee houses and then the hippie drop-outs in San Francisco.

'Hipster' came to be used to describe middle-class kids who were interested in the alternative scene, whether that was indie or techno. As opposed to the yuppies of the 1980s, the modern hipster was less flashy and materialistic. They didn't spend their money on expensive cars and designer clothes, but instead bought the latest electronic products, cool vintage pieces and tattoos. Music and film were downloaded and TV series were streamed. While they

Hipster style, Lovebox Festival, London, 2010

used social media and online streaming, hipsters also paid tribute to analogue with cassettes, early 1980s gaming and an appreciation of vinyl. The Polaroid camera made a comeback as the original way to take a selfie, particularly with Instagram recreating the Polaroid photo look with hazy 1970s filters.

This embracing of new technology and nostalgia for the old was mixed with a concern for the environment by cycling, recycling and upcycling. The fixed-wheel bike became a signifier of the hipster, originating from bike messengers – a defined culture and community in itself – and where particular bikes demonstrated a specialist, insider knowledge and cool status.

The hipster demographic often shared flats, or even bedrooms, due to rocketing rent prices in major cities, and moved out to cheaper working-class areas like Shoreditch and Dalston in London, or Brooklyn in New York. These areas were then deemed desirable, cool, and became more expensive on the back of this new population moving in. Portland, Oregon was one of the first cities to see the rise of the new ethical consumerist who made money from the dot com industry and TV show *Portlandia* affectionately poked fun at its breed of hipsters. In Brooklyn, the Bedford Avenue bike lane runs through every ethnic enclave, reflecting a change in demographic. Spike Lee criticised the gentrification of Brooklyn: 'Why does it take an influx of white New Yorkers for the facilities to get better?' he asked.

Roskilde Festival, Denmark, 2013 Normcore couple, Brick Lane, London, 2009

2002
Electroclash in Brooklyn

2005
London's
Shoreditch
developed

HIPSTER

Mumford and Sons
indie-folk
2009

2008
Economic depression

Normcore
2013

Hipsters had a desire to find something unique and alternative amongst the acceptably cool. It was a look that was hip and forward, but also nostalgic. They borrowed from hippies, grunge, punk and hip hop and fused them together, in a melting pot of styles and trends. 'Instead of creating a culture of their own, hipsters proved content to borrow from trends long past,' wrote *Time* magazine. They dressed with an overstyled casualness in grungy check shirts and floral dresses from Urban Outfitters, brightly coloured v-neck t-shirts from American Apparel, Wayfarers, Converse all-stars and baseball caps. There was a trend for the bright, tribal prints of early 1990s hip-hop artists DJ Jazzy Jeff and the Fresh Prince and Salt-N-Pepa, and the Wham 'Club Tropicana' look of the 1980s with colourful denim shorts, as seen with electroclash.

The idea of being the most authentic was also important, finding new 'undiscovered' places in the world to visit, as DJ and producer Diplo boasted of searching out rare sounds in Latin American danger zones. Being ironic became another signifier of the hipster – they would appropriate something kitsch or considered bad taste, such as wearing a wife-beater vest or sporting a porn-star moustache, or a trucker cap despite having no connection to long-haul driving. By wearing something ironically, they were knowingly winking at its ridiculousness. 'Whether reinforcing sexism through the use of ironic rhetoric or questioning dominant culture, irony plays a distinctive role in how hipsters are perceived,' wrote Kristofor R. Vogel, from the University of Texas.

Just like punk and grunge before it, the label hipster became mainstream and was then used as an insult for those with a particular haircut or style of

ABOVE A young, bearded and tattooed hipster, Shoreditch, London

dress. Advertising agencies were often based in creative, hipster enclaves, and so their tastes would inevitably seep into adverts, particularly their favoured music choice of electro. Sleeve tattoos spread out of Shoreditch and Brooklyn and on to the arms of footballers. Trendy hipster diners served foraged foods, cocktails in jam jars or kitsch cereal from around the world. Taylor Swift even sang of 'dressing up like hipsters' in her 2012 song '22', wearing an ironic t-shirt and bowler hat in the music video.

TV series *Girls*, written by and starring Lena Dunham, depicts the new generation for the 2010s living in New York – instead of *Sex and the City's* cosmopolitans in Manhattan, it's Pabst Blue Ribbon beer in Brooklyn. Dunham's character, Hannah, is a Brooklyn hipster girl, with Eloise tattoos and

ink done by one of her best friends. She regularly appears nude, undone and with a feminist pride in revealing all her flaws. With classic hipster irony, Hannah makes jokes about date rape to avoid exposing herself to real fears of failure. Dunham herself is self-aware and recognised that her show had the 'rarified white hipster thing'.

Matt Granfield, in his book *HipsterMattic*, sums it up when he argues with his friend that he is not a hipster. 'Dave pointed out the fact that I wore thick-rimmed Ray Ban Wayfarer style reading glasses, Converse sneakers, a bicycle courier-style bag, which usually had a copy of a classic American novel in it, that I worked in advertising as a day job, and I spent an inordinate amount of time tweeting about photography exhibitions.'

STEAMPUNK

With corsets, tweed and ray guns, steampunk pays tribute to a science fiction vision of the Victorian era through literature, fashion, design and graphic novels. It's a creative movement based on the perspective of how the Victorians imagined the future and its technologies to be, and where followers create spectacular inventions and costumes from found objects.

It's in the Victorian science fiction stories of H.G. Wells and Jules Verne – the technology and imagined worlds that have inspired and shaped steampunk. The word 'steampunk' combines the DIY nature of punk with technology at the time of steam power and was coined by science fiction writer K.W. Jeter in 1987. It's an elegant, aristocratic fashion that harks back to the romanticism of another era – a sepia-toned, rust-brown world rather than the dark, macabre mourning clothes of the goth, as if the image has been caught by an old Victorian camera.

The nineteenth century saw an industrial revolution that created a sense that anything was possible. The Victorians still held a wonder in exploration, as it was a time when people travelled on long and tiring journeys by sea or rail, where airships were things of imagined beauty and a telescope was the only way to venture into space. This sense of adventure was depicted in the pages of *Around the World in 80 Days*, or in Rudyard Kipling's exotic stories of India. It is this nostalgia for an era of exploration and inventions, a time before airplanes made it so much easier, that fuels the steampunk creativity. 'Quaint to some eyes, or outright bizarre, steampunk fashion is compelling all the same. It is that rarity, a phenomenon with the potential to capture a wider audience, offering a genteel and disciplined alternative to both the slack look of hip-hop and the menacing spirit of goth,' wrote the *New York Times*.

The original steampunks were those of the nineteenth century who fantasised about what the future would be like. Mary Shelley's *Frankenstein*, published in 1818, imagined how electricity could jump-start an artificial human with transplanted organs. French writer Jules Verne, in his series of *Voyages Extraordinaires*, created immense adventures deep under sea and into

PREVIOUS PAGE Steampunk cosplayers, Festival del Fumetto, Milan, 2014 ABOVE The annual Wave-Gotik-Treffen music festival, Leipzig, 2014

the earth's core, with dream-like technologies of the future such as submarines made from bronze and airships powered with fins.

The 1960 film version of H.G. Wells *The Time Machine* recreated his world with a Victorian feel instead of the usual shiny, futuristic design. The time machine was mahogany and leather, and the inventor wore a Victorian suit as he travelled through time; a combination that really reflects the mood and feel of steampunk. It is as if inventions have been created by madcap professors in the wood-panelled rooms of Victorian London homes.

The 1980s saw a new cult literary genre for science fiction, romanticising Victorian London and its streets lit by gas lamps, its mahogany interiors and repressive but ornate costumes. By the 1990s this genre would expand into fashion and inventions.

The movement grew from the way people could share their ideas and designs over the internet and in blogs, encouraging the explosion of steampunk. Artists and designers have created highly intricate designs and technological contraptions along with the fashions on display at conventions and festivals.

Steampunk was also encouraged by *Doctor Who*, films like *The League of Extraordinary Gentlemen* and Guy Ritchie's *Sherlock Holmes*. The post-apocalyptic scavengers in *Mad Max*, with their contraptions and costumes fashioned from pieces of scrap metal and brown leather, added a dangerous, rougher edge to the style. The 2011 *Three Musketeers* film was set in a 'clockpunk' world – Renaissance-era science fiction.

Just as Victorian science fiction depicted time machines and other fantastical designs, real and imagined technologies from the Victorian era

ABOVE Vaporosa Mente event held in Turin, 2014

are invented and created by steampunks. Coffee machines are fashioned to look as if steam-powered, pretend weapons are modelled as if from an apocalypse and mobile phones and tablets can be given a steampunk make-over with a brass and cog effect. 'If the Victorians had access to all of our new technology, it would be done in beautiful woods, brass rivets and there'd be an exposed mechanical element to all of the devices,' said Art Donovan, steampunk curator at the Museum of the History of Science, Oxford University.

Steampunk fashions combine neo-Victorian, Edwardian and military style with brass goggles, harnesses and clockwork pendants, and a ray gun held at the hip. Costumes use cogs, bolts, brass piping and screws to bring these technologies into fashion. As well as Victorian costumes, steampunk can also be based on fashions from other lands in the nineteenth century – Japan, India, the Wild West. Will Smith's *Wild Wild West* was a 1990s steampunk film that combined Victorian Wild West fashions with fantastical technology. Japanese animation, with its goggle-wearing hackers, is also a plundered fashion source.

Steampunk men wear explorer's helmets and brass goggles, Dr Watson tweeds, Mad Hatter top hats, and elaborate *Mad Max* style gas masks. They have the appearance of a gentleman cowboy in a leather trench or frock coat, or an aristocrat in a waistcoat.

Steampunk fashion for women is sculpted with bustles, corsets and crinolines, imitating the way Victorian dress was built up to shape the female body. They wear voluminous, Scarlett O'Hara gowns and corsets, but punked up with combat boots and dyed hair. Inspiration also comes from Amelia

2012
Lady Gaga goes steampunk

Burning Man Festival

1987   1999   STEAMPUNK   2007   2015

'Steampunk' coined   *League of Extraordinary*   *Mad Max: Fury Road* released
                      Gentlemen graphic novel

CLOCKWISE, FROM TOP LEFT Coachella Festival, 2015; Whitby Goth Weekend; Burning Man Festival, 2005

Earhart goggles and aviator caps, or the Mata Hari spy in steampunk graphic novel *Alter Nation*. Women become heroines of their own fiction, with crinoline constructions exposed without fabric, a weapon in their garter or at their hip, an eye-piece with telescopic lens or a mechanical arm and leather holster, like Charlize Theron in *Mad Max: Fury Road*.

Diana M. Pho in *Anatomy of Steampunk* says: 'A sense of high-flying adventure, discovery, invention, and elaborate theatricality are intrinsic to steampunk outfits. . . . Metalwork and leather combined with satin and lace. Warm browns and creams mix alongside vibrant colours. Bustle skirts and tailcoats fit in with gritty shirtsleeves or ripped fishnets. Bowlers, top hats, pageboys, pith helmets and aviator caps adorn the heads of men and women alike in a shared sense of play.'

Steampunk followers search out their outfits at vintage shops and scour flea markets, choosing fingerless gloves, bowler hats, frock coats and high-necked blouses with lace. They find cogs and watch parts on eBay or create their own fantastical pieces to sell on Etsy. Steampunk hats can be lavish creations with feathers added to a top hat or percher, with clock pieces and chains. Online boutiques allow people to buy designs from all over the world – Clockwork Couture, Festooned Butterfly, KMK designs – selling hand-crafted corsets, bustles and crinolines. In Pakistan in 2011, designer Ali Fateh created a steampunk collection with bags and jewellery, where actress Aamina Sheikh modelled them fashioned as a steampunk heroine.

Steampunk crossed from a subculture of people meeting at festivals and conventions, to haute couture fashion inspiration, first seen in Vivienne Westwood's 1988 Time Machine collection. Alexander McQueen is one design house closely associated with steampunk and in 2012 models were dressed in corsets and crinolines, constructed veils over their faces. Lady Gaga's out-there costumes also incorporated steampunk glasses and corsetry.

One aspect of steampunk that differentiates it from other subcultures is that it's not necessarily for the young. In fact many of its followers and creators are in their thirties, forties and fifties. But it also fits with the look of hipsters; their beards, tweeds and moustaches and a hankering for past technologies; and steampunk permeates into youth festivals and a London fancy dress ball called White Mischief. A forty-foot steampunk treehouse was exhibited at the Burning Man festival in 2007, and the festival, along with Coachella, has attracted *Mad Max* versions of steampunks in skimpy costumes and leather contraptions.

Robert Brown from Abney Park, a steampunk band which began as a goth band, told the *Guardian*: 'We're living in a world where everything is a beige plastic box, so going back to a world that was elegant and beautiful has an appeal.'

HARAJUKU STYLE

Harajuku is the fashion lover's district of Tokyo, a pedestrian shopping paradise where quirky style tribes display their individuality, often following the concept of kawaii – a Japanese word for cute.

Kawaii is embodied in Lolita kei, a subculture emerging on the streets of Osaka, and then Harajuku in the 1990s, where girls in their late teens and twenties began dressing in Rococo and Victorian confections, like sugary Bo Peeps loaded with accessories. They dressed in Red Riding Hood capes, bell-shaped skirts that came to the knee and ruffled blouses, bloomers and parasols, as if taken straight from Victorian dolls. As well as traditional Lolita, there are other variations including punk Lolita, sweet Lolita, with berry and cupcake imagery, and wa Lolita, which incorporates Japanese tradition. A darker twist on the cute style is gothic Lolita, or goshikku roriita, with black gothic bride dresses, crosses and dark make-up, and, around 2005, a trend for staining smocks and faces with fake blood.

Like punks, they made up their own rules, creating and borrowing ideas to come up with something that was completely unique. Instead of designer labels like Vivienne Westwood and Comme des Garçons, they wore specialist boutique brands like Milk and Angelic Pretty, and aimed to carry themselves with elegance and modesty. The culture really flourished in the late 1990s when girls would gather outside Harajuku station, in front of Yoyogi Park and in the LeForet department store to display and compare their costumes and later post pictures online.

Kawaii is a way of retreating back to childhood, to escape from responsibility and the cruelty of adult life, with Hello Kitty as one of the most popular brands in Japan since its introduction in 1974. It extends beyond the Lolita look with the decora kei in Harajuku. They incorporate kitsch imagery of cookies and candy, animal prints and manga or anime characters, with an overload of accessories in rainbow bright colours, including hair clips, bows and ribbons.

Harajuku has, for many years, been the alternative, quirky area of Tokyo for teenagers. After the Second World War, Japan was occupied for six and a half years by American troops, and in Tokyo the American area was centred around Harajuku. Those Japanese who lived near the barracks had greater access to American clothes, showing its early origins as a trendsetting centre.

In 2002, the *New York Times* described how the Harajuku scene was only possible 'in a country whose isolationist history endowed its inhabitants with the ability to take anything material the world had to offer and to transform it into something their own.'

Fashionable Japanese youths began borrowing elements of western subcultures and in the 1950s the media began referring to zoku, or tribes, of youth cultures. At that time, the taiyozoku, or sun tribe, wore Aloha shirts and shorts, and were named after a popular novel of the same name, with a sequel called *Crazy Fruits*. There was a 1960s mod style cult with angular haircuts and A-line dresses, and the kaminarizoku, or thunder tribe, of the 1970s wore leathers and rode motorbikes.

From the late 1970s Harajuku was the place for teenagers to hang out when two of the streets were closed to traffic on Sundays, allowing them to listen to bands and watch street performers like the rockers with their pompadours, dancing to Jerry Lee Lewis, or the Bronx b-boys who visited on a world tour in 1983. The area also became a meeting place for the bamboo shoot tribe, or takenoko-zoku, who wore colourful unisex silk traditional costumes and would dance in groups with swinging arm

movements. These street performers and fashion-conscious teenagers began wearing clothes that were more outrageous, captured by street photographer Shiochi Aoki for *Street* in 1985 and *Fruits* from 1997.

Japanese elegance had long been appreciated by designers like Paul Poiret, who incorporated hobble skirts and kimonos in his turn-of-the-century designs, but Japanese designers experienced a revolution in the 1980s. Comme des Garçons and Issey Miyake brought new technologies and styles to fashion, with Japan considered a futurist country with a rapid economic development, consumerism and excellence in technology. In 1983, *Vogue* called Japanese fashion 'the freer spirit' and 'more experimental' than its western counterpart.

When the economy crashed in the early 1990s, it caused an uncertainty as Japan's working population were not guaranteed a job for life, and the country experienced a wave of depression. It was then that individual youth style really exploded, while also signifying a return to childish things.

Lolitas were partly inspired by the Rococo and Victorian costumes worn by popular Japanese visual kei bands in the mid-1990s, including Moi Dix Mois and Malice Mizer with their dramatic goth make-up. The visuals and costumes of these bands were as important as the music, and their fans started dressing like them. 'Gothic in Europe is pretty fearsome and dirty and has aggression, but in Japanese Lolita it has been "sweetified". And punk in Lolita doesn't have that anti-society feel that it has in Britain,' Rupert Faulkner, curator of a V&A Lolita exhibition, told the *Tokyo Times*.

ABOVE Students in pastel sweet Lolita fashion, Harajuku, 2015 RIGHT Street style, Harajuku, 2009

The Bamboo Shoot tribe
1979

1995

HARAJUKU
STYLE

Fruits magazine
1997

2004
Gwen Stefani's Harajuku girls

Malice Mizer
visual kei band

2001
Angelic Pretty

LEFT Matching outfits, Harajuku, 2013

Despite the name Lolita, and a pervading 'Lolita' complex in Japanese culture, they were not sexually suggestive, rather innocent and elegant – owing more to *Alice in Wonderland* than geisha. Their full skirts, long socks and Mary Jane shoes from brands like Baby, The Stars Shine Bright, and Alice and the Pirates created a fantasy world of fairytales. It allowed them to express themselves outside of school and work, as well as providing a sense of protection from the overly sexualised and pressured adult environment.

Fashion became a way of life and self-expression. A Lolita, Aiko, told the *Sunday Times* in 2005: 'I never feel self-conscious in anything I wear. If I did, I'd look terrible. When I'm in my look, I'm telling the world that I like feeling beautiful and that I'm not going to just go and work in an office for the rest of my life.' *The Gothic and Lolita Bible*, a magazine and book hybrid dedicated to the movement, helped standardise the look and featured lifestyle tips like patterns for making costumes and accessories, and recipes for gothic tea parties, such as chocolate cakes with sugar crosses.

Entering into the twenty-first century, Lolita and kawaii fashion began receiving international attention. When Gwen Stefani was promoting her debut album in 2004, four professional dancers acting as Harajuku girls were constantly by her side,

and she used a Lolita-esque *Alice in Wonderland* theme in the 'What You Waiting For?' video. Stefani had become fascinated with Japanese street style on a visit to Tokyo in 1996. 'Everyone had this crazy personal style,' she said. 'The last couple of times I was there, it had evolved into all these different things like the gothic Lolitas and girls with blonde hair and dark tans and high heels, like they were from Hollywood . . . I did a shout-out to them: "Harajuku girls, you got the wicked style." That's when the dream started.' It wasn't just Stefani who took on the Lolita look – Courtney Love co-wrote a manga-inspired comic book about Princess Ai, a character similar to Love, but dressed in a gothic and Lolita style.

The emergence of cosplay around Jingu Bridge often appears as a crossover with Lolita fashion, with followers dressed up as their favourite characters. The gothic Lolita look is also not too far removed from the waitresses at maid cafes in the Akihabara district. They dress in black-and-white frilled dresses to wait on male customers, pretending that they are welcoming home their master.

But in Harajuku, the Lolita and kawaii style is still very much evident at LeForet, in boutiques and brands including Maison de Julietta, and with popular *Alice in Wonderland* tea parties held by fashion brands and Lolita followers.

SAPEUR

Amongst the war-ruined buildings and shanty town slums of Brazzaville, the capital of the Republic of the Congo, and Kinshasa, capital of the Democratic Republic of the Congo, the sapeurs, or 'la sape', stand out as peacocks defying their circumstances, with a gentlemanly code to their style of dress and behaviour. La sape is an acronym for the Societe des Ambianceurs et des Personnes Elegantes, translated as the Society of Tastemakers and Elegant People, and with their French flare and style, they were also given the nickname 'le Parisiens'.

Brazzaville and Kinshasa are set over the river from one other, just a ten-minute ferry ride apart, but the DRC is often considered one of the most dangerous countries in the world, and according to World Bank statistics, one of the poorest. Brazzaville is the smaller, comparatively wealthier and more stable city, but still with a low average income. Despite the poverty, the sapeurs dress in expensive designer suits of periwinkle blue, candy pink and lemon yellow, with polished crocodile skin loafers and bowler hats.

It's an all-encompassing way of life, and sapeur rules of dress include only wearing three colours, along with white, at the same time. Pocket squares are on display, an umbrella or cane is carried, and there's an extensive grooming routine in a country with limited water supplies. Followers call it 'sapologie', and it's been passed down through generations, beginning with the houseboys who mimicked the French colonials during the 1920s, but wore the clothes as flamboyantly as possible. Professor Didier Gondola, an authority on culture and history in West Africa, recounted a sapeur telling him of 'our fathers and our grandfathers who were servants in white mens' homes and were often paid with clothing. My father was an elegant man . . . the kind of person to put a breast pocket on his pyjamas.' It was reminiscent of the African-American slaves who created their own styles from the clothes given to them by the slave owners in America, and 'were only too keen to display, even to flaunt, their finery both to other slaves and to whites,' as described in the book *Stylin': African American Expressive Culture*.

It may be an expensive style to maintain, but the sapeurs borrow and swap pieces, select items from local shops or have an item made up to their specification by a tailor. In 1988, the *New York Times* reported on the sapeurs who were hanging out by the river in Brazzaville, posing in their finery. Groups of young Congolese lived in Paris's eighteenth arrondissement for parts of the year, before travelling back to the Congo armed with 'Yves Saint Laurent suits, Yamamoto jackets, Marcel Lassance suits, Gresson shoes, Cacharel pants'. One sapeur told the paper of his visits to Paris in late July and early August to catch the end of summer sales to snap up bargains which he would then sell on back home.

It's said that a sapeur should be gentle and against war and fighting, and must show kindness and civility. Their way of dress also changes their manner and stance, and they perform with a different gait, propping themselves in motion with their cane, elbows and knees at angles. As noted by writer and professor Peter H. Wood, historic dance in the culture around the Congo involved bent knees and elbows, following a West African belief that 'straightened knees, hips and elbows epitomised death and rigidity, while flexed joints embodied energy and life.'

The origins of sapeur style can be traced back to the French and Belgian colonisation of the Bakongo kingdoms in the late nineteenth century. From around 1884 the DRC (formerly Zaire) was personally owned by King Leopold and exploited for rubber and ivory to such a horrifying extent that the Belgian government annexed it from him. The Republic of the Congo became a French colony from the 1880s, and in 1908 it would form part of French Equatorial Africa with Brazzaville as the capital.

The first sapeur is considered to be André Matsoua, who lived in Paris in the 1920s and returned to the Congo dressed in European finery as an outspoken voice against French colonialism. He demanded French citizenship for everyone within its territories and was imprisoned by the rulers of French Equatorial Africa in 1942. As the capital of the French colonies, Brazzaville became a haven for the bourgeoisie during the Second World War, and

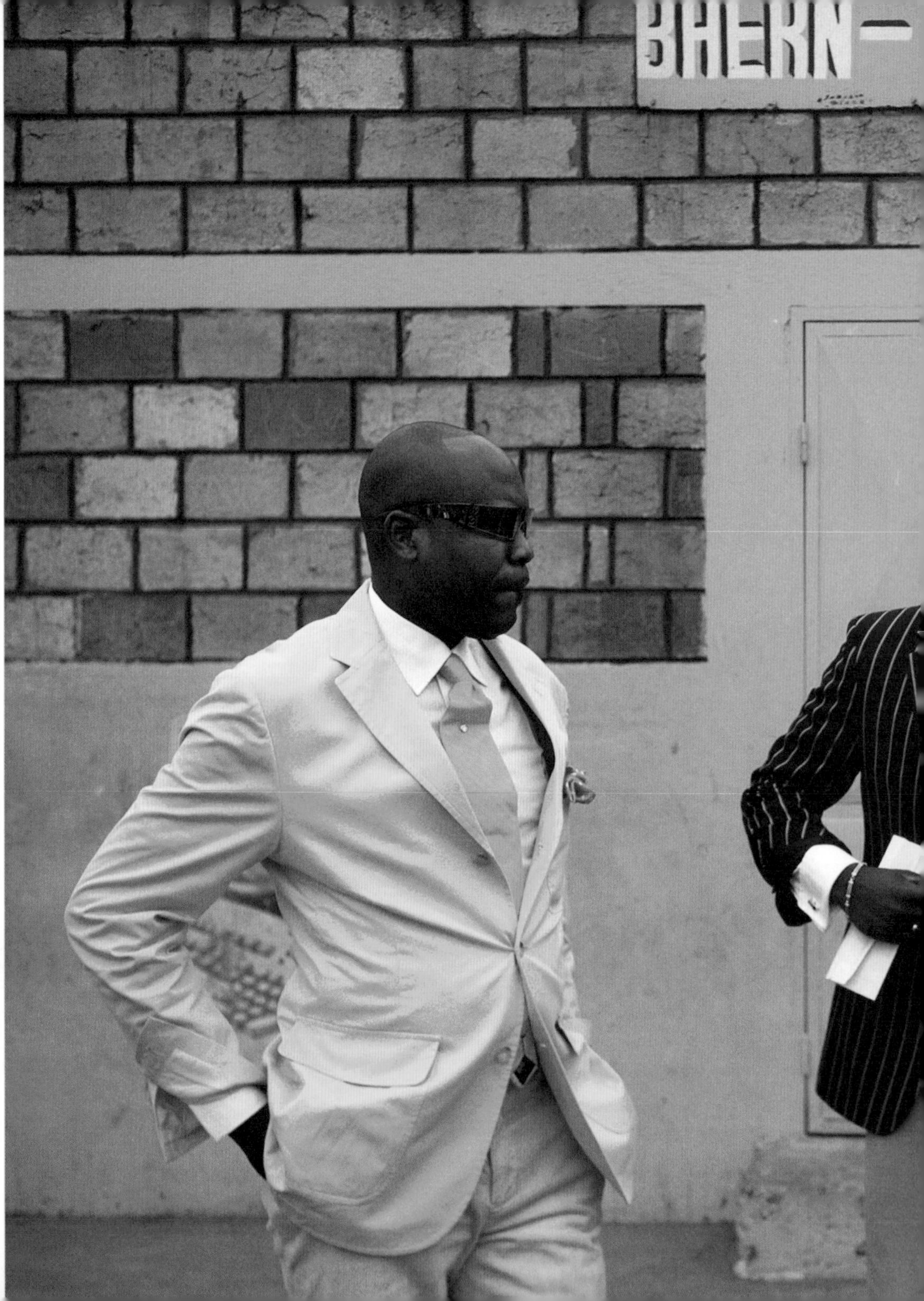

ERVICES
MTN
Photocopie
Saisie
lastification
anner
aintenance
avure - CD

they would show off their tailored, elegant clothing. While colonialism repressed local customs, groups of Congolese imitated the French with their elegant dress in an act of defiance, as had been the case in the early days of European presence. John Thornton, in *Africa and Africans in the Making of the Atlantic World*, noted that following European discovery of Africa, 'rulers and the elite in Congo quickly took to European fashion . . . so that by the mid-seventeenth century the possession of European style of clothing was a sign of status.'

Brazzaville is surrounded by hot and humid tropical rainforest and situated on the banks of the Congo, and so in the early days of the sapeur, the streets were often a muddy hazard for walking in expensive shoes, and sapeurs would hire men to pushcart them across the streets.

Both countries gained independence in 1960, and the Congolese could travel to Paris and return with the latest fashions, Yves Saint Laurent being a particular favourite. In the DRC in the 1970s, following political upheaval, it was forbidden by President Mobutu Sese Seko to wear western suits, and instead the population wore tunics that broke from the colonial past, and were called abacost, short for *à bas le costume* – literally 'down with the suit'. He renamed the country Zaire as a way to claim back African values and culture. Rebels would defy his brutal dictatorship by wearing suits, while musician Papa Wemba formed his own French-inspired fashion cult, which he called La Sape. They were 'a group as obsessively fashion-conscious as the British mods had been in the 1960s', as reported by *The Times* in 2004. Wemba would sing on one of his tracks, 'Don't give up the clothes. It's our religion,' and the sapeur style of Kinshasa would diverge into a more eclectic, less rule-driven style with leather, multiple colours and patterns.

The DRC would be torn apart by civil war and human atrocity, but German artist Carsten Holler recalled, from his first visit in 2001, that 'Kinshasa is electric, filled with music, sapeurs . . . and live concerts, like no other town I have seen.'

1910
French Equatorial Africa
established

SAPEUR

1960
Congo independence

Mobutu bans
western clothing

1971

2014

Sapeurs feature in Guinness advert

LEFT Sapeur Patience Moutala, Brazzaville, 2014 BOTTOM LEFT Sapeurs in Kinshasa, 2012

As for the Republic of Congo, in 1988, the *New York Times* reported: 'Initially, the government clashed with the sapeurs. More recently, it has adopted a laissez-faire attitude. When traveling overseas, Congo's President, Denis Sassou Nguesso, routinely changes his army fatigues for an Yves Saint Laurent suit.'

Didier Gondola asserts that 'the sapeur is also about masculinity, politics, changing the stereotypes about how people view Africa. It's about a lot of things, about beating the West at its own game, which is fashion: "You colonised us but we dress better than you."'

A 2014 Guinness advert featuring the sapeurs depicted their metamorphosis as they shed their working clothes for a polished, smart sartorial style. One of the sapeurs featured, Hassan Salvador, described working as a warehouse manager and spending twenty per cent of his salary on clothes. Feron Ngouabi, a fireman, recounted how he spent all his earnings on clothes, subsidising his income with the two taxis that he owns.

Sapeurs gather at La Main Bleue, Brazzaville, a bar near to the banks of the River Congo where they sip on a beer and display their fine clothing. In 2011, the *Wall Street Journal* described the scene, where 'the streets and alleyways outside the bar are made of dirt, littered with refuse and remains, and lined by tin-topped shacks. A gauntlet of kids and adults forms spontaneously as soon as the sapeurs start stepping out of taxis and cars to enter the bar. The crowd stares at them in wonder, shouting out the names of some of the well-known sapeurs as they recognise them walking by.'

KOGAL

Youth styles in Japan flourished in the 1990s, with distinctive, individual looks that took western fashions, twisted them with unique Japanese touches, and went wild. One of the most prevalent was a fashion movement based around 'girl' or 'gal' culture in the Shibuya district of Tokyo, with a flagrant display of fashion brands and consumerism, and founded on a fetishised schoolgirl look.

Shibuya is the ultra-trendy entertainment district of Tokyo with nightlife, karaoke bars, huge neon signs and video screens, the 'pedestrian scramble crossroads' and shopping centre Shibuya 109, catering to girls in their teens and twenties. It was here, in the 1990s, that kogal, or kogyaru, style was developed.

'Gyaru' means girl, originally coming from a brand of Wrangler Gal jeans in 1972, and would become a self-referential suffix for different girl types. 'Ko' is translated as young or immature, so the word kogyaru or kogal means 'high-school girl' or 'young girl.' Gals who mimicked California surf style with blonde hair, tans and aloha prints were known as surfer gyaru, and it was this style that influenced kogal fashion, along with pop star Amuro Namie, with her American-inspired look.

Kogals promoted a valley girl aesthetic of fake tan, bleached blonde or chestnut hair, and where girls from wealthy families could rebel by wearing their school uniform in a sexualised way. With a concept of ero kawaii, meaning erotic and cute, they wore their school uniform of plaid or pleated skirt (changed from the sailor uniform in the 1980s) with long white socks, cute, cartoonish accessories and visible bra straps. Some even hitched up their skirts so short they exposed their pants, wearing another pair over the top to preserve modesty. With their weejun loafers and bulky socks, the emphasis on their bare thighs would be a focus for the lecherous side of Japanese society. By the end of the 1990s the kogal schoolgirl was at the heart of Japanese pop culture.

As it became more popular, kogal developed into a more extreme ganguro style from 1999, using tanning machines and lotions to make their skin as dark as possible. It would be accentuated with white eye-shadow and lips, hair bleached and teased, huge platform Spice Girl style boots, very short skirts, neon colours and gold jewellery. With such strange appearances they were given the name 'yamanba', or mountain witch, after a children's folk tale.

In Japan, school uniforms have long been treated as a fetishised symbol of rebellion in films, comics and anime such as Sailor Moon manga. The European sailor-style uniform had been introduced in the nineteenth century, following the Meiji Restoration in 1868, which opened up contact between Japan and the western world.

Sukeban, meaning bad girl or delinquent, emerged as a character in the 1970s and 1980s, wearing a school uniform with dyed hair and colour-ed socks. In 1981 Hiroko Yakushimaru in *Sailor Suit and Machine Gun* played a schoolgirl who kills members of a rival gang. In *Battle Royale* school-girls dressed in their uniform of blazers and pleated skirts are forced to fight each other to the death, and in Quentin Tarantino's *Kill Bill*, Go Go Yubari is a psychotic assassin schoolgirl.

The 1980s were the 'bubble years' as the economy boomed, and Japanese consumers obsessed over luxury brands like Louis Vuitton and Chanel, becoming part of a visual conformity of Japanese tradition and new western behaviour. Kogal would

also derive from, and be seen as the little sisters of, the bodycon, or bodikon gyaru, where female office workers in the late 1980s would wear tight, figure hugging dresses by Azzedine Alaia, Herve Leger and Thierry Mugler, and accessorise with feather boas and luxury shoes and handbags. They wore their hair long and dyed, with little curled fringes, and at Juliana's nightclub in Tokyo, they would display themselves on the highest stage, signalling to look but not touch. After the bubble burst, and Japan entered into a period of economic uncertainty, fashion editorials focused on brands like Gap and Levi. The kogal girls in Shibuya made alternative statements by casually carrying a Chanel bag or a Burberry scarf – a look of wealthy indifference. Kogal would be a driving force for consumerism in the 1990s and their influence led to major trends such as using pagers and text messages before they became widely available.

Their social life was based around Shibuya station, which became their stage. They would gather at karaoke bars or at shopping malls, have their photos taken in purikura booths and use the photo stickers to decorate objects or exchange amongst friends. Shibuya, by 1998, was swarming with kogyaru girls, buying products at Shibuya 109 directly marketed to them, or finding style tips in *Egg*, a street magazine for kogals and written by kogals, starting out in 1995. There was also a chance they could be spotted by style photographers from fashion magazines like *Fruits*.

1999
Yamanba style

1981

1990

KOGAL

1995

Ageha tribe
2008

Sailor Suit and Machine Gun released

Bodicon fashion becomes popular

Egg fashion magazine

Like the California girl of the 1995 film *Clueless*, kogals created their own speech and way of communicating, which often used English loan words. They were the first to develop emoticons, or kao moji (face characters) using punctuation and accents to create emotions like the smiley or an 'ouch' face.

'During the 1990s the mainstream media incited a moral panic over kogals, amplifying their perceived deviant behaviours and language,' wrote Laura Miller in her essay on the kogals. One of the more shocking aspects was enjo kosai, or subsidised companionship, where kogals accepted payment from businessmen to go on group dates, mostly to a karaoke box. They saw themselves as exploiting the 'disgusting' men, and would have fun phoning into terekura 'telephone clubs', places near train hubs where men would connect to girls through a party line.

They had a contradictory sexualised behaviour where they would meet boyfriends at love hotels, while also having a fondness for Hello Kitty bags and purses, and would constantly be propositioned by men around the Shibuya district. Girls would exploit the sleaziness by selling their used underwear to the men who were titillated by this schoolgirl look, and it led to some kogals being seen as synonymous with prostitutes. A former kogal recounted to *Tokyo Damage Report*: 'If you had blonde hair and loose socks, everyone looked at you like you were a teenage prostitute. If you went to 7/11 the clerks would accuse you of stealing, even if you hadn't taken anything.'

Kogal made an extreme shift from 1999, with the ganguro, translated as 'face black', turning the kogal's appeal to men on its head. The style shocked and repulsed, as well as challenged feminine norms by creating an unnatural appearance with deep tan make-up, white lips and eyes, and silver or orange hair. Some described it as an imitation of African-American culture with the incorporation of African elements through the use of darkened makeup and animal patterns such as tiger or zebra prints. However it was a completely

A ganguro in Shibuya district, 2003

unique appearance partly owing to the working-class girls who were now imitating the wealthier kogal. Their look was so strange 'that few boys of the same age were attracted to them, and although the girls often walked around in the streets, boys kept at a distance,' wrote Yuniya Kawamura in *Japan Fashion Now*. 'The girls didn't care about outsiders' judgments; rather, it was more important for them to gain respect from other girls with the same tastes.'

Ganguro petered out after 2001 and the sight of gyaru in Shibuya became less common. Gals would tone down their looks, and by 2008 a glamorous blonde tribe called ageha appeared, common in the Tokyo hostess clubs. A group of kuro gyaru, which translates as 'black skin gals', emerged in 2011, paying tribute to ganguro with less extreme tanned skin, nails decorated elaborately, hair dyed lavender or blonde, and with a clubber look of furry boots and denim shorts bought from 109 shop DIA. A gyaru told *Tokyo Fashion*: 'There are many kinds of gyaru, but we prefer dark skin so we go to tanning salons almost every day.'

Tokyo's districts have long been popular with street-style photographers who are guaranteed to capture a quirky and completely original look, like no other place in the world. Japan's young people express themselves through wearing high-end fashion, adopting visual-kei, with its punk and goth stylings, or acting out fantasies through costume – including manga or superhero-inspired cosplay, dolly-kei, with a look based on European fairy-tales, and the Mori girl, dressed as if she came from the forest.

Select Bibliography

General

Brewster, Bill and Broughton, Frank, *Last Night a DJ Saved My Life: The History of the Disc Jockey* (Headline, 2006)

Cohen, Stanley, *Folk Devils and Moral Panics* (Routledge Classics, 2011)

Hebdige, Dick, *Subculture: The Meaning of Style* (Routledge, 1979)

Maconie, Stuart, *Cider with Roadies* (Ebury Publishing, 2005)

Melly, George, *Revolt into Style: The Pop Arts* (Faber & Faber, 2013)

Reynolds, Simon, *Energy Flash: A Journey Through Rave Music and Dance Culture* (Faber & Faber, 2013)

Savage, Jon, *Teenage: The Creation of Youth 1875 to 1945* (Chatto & Windus, 2007)

Steele, Valerie, Mears, Patricia, Kawamuram, Yuniya and Narushi, Hiroshi *Japan Fashion Now*, (Fashion Institute of Technology, Yale University Press, 2010)

Taylor, D J, *Bright Young People: The Rise and Fall of a Generation 1918–1940* (Random House, 2010)

Westwood, Vivienne and Kelly, Ian, *Vivienne Westwood* (Pan Macmillan, 2014)

White, Shane and White, Graham, *Stylin': African American Expressive Culture, From its Beginnings to the Zoot Suit* (Cornell University Press, 1998)

Flapper

'The 1920 Girl', *The Times*, 5 February 1920

Cox, Caroline, *1920s Style: How to Get the Look of the Decade* (Carlton Books, 2013)

'Flapper Dictionary', *The Flapper*, July 1922

Lavine, W Robert, *In a Glamorous Fashion: The Fabulous Years of Hollywood Costume Design* (Charles Scribner's Sons, 1980)

Mackrell, Judith, *Flappers: Six Women of a Dangerous Generation* (Pan Macmillan, 2013)

Moore, Lucy, *Anything Goes: A Biography of the Roaring Twenties* (Atlantic Books, 2008)

Harlem Renaissance

Garber, Eric, 'A Spectacle in Colour, the Lesbian and Gay Subculture of Jazz Age Harlem' in *Hidden from History: Reclaiming the Gay and Lesbian Past* (New American Library, 1989)

'I'd like to Show you Harlem!', *Independent*, April 1921

The Zoot suit

'Los Angeles Zoot: Race "Riot", the Pachuco and Black Music Culture', Douglas Henry Daniels, *Journal of Negro History*, vol. 82, no. 2, 1997

Swing Kid

Kater, Michael H, *Different Drummers: Jazz in the culture of Nazi Germany* (Oxford University Press, 1992)

'Swing is the Thing in Germany', *New York Times*, 14 November 1937

'Swing Music in New York', *The Times*, 18 January 1938

Beatnik

'Cool Cats Don't Dig Squares', Harry T. Moore, *New York Times*, 24 May 1959

'Defiant Fashions for a Beatnik Heiress', *New York Times*, 24 May 1960

'Elegy for a Desolation Angel', Lester Bangs, *Rolling Stone*, 29 November 1969

George-Warren, Holly, *The Rolling Stone Book of the Beats* (Bloomsbury, 1990)

'Jack Kerouac, Aftermath: The Philosophy of the Beat Generation', *Esquire*, March 1958

Teddy boy

Ferris, Ray and Lord, Julian, *Teddy Boys, A Concise History* (Milo Books, 2012)

Steel-Perkins, Chris and Smith, Richard, *The Teds* (Dewi Lewis Publishing, 1979)

'Youth Hits Back', *Daily Mirror*, 27 September 1956

Greaser & Rocker

Marcus, Daniel, *Happy Days and Wonder Years: The Fifties and Sixties in Contemporary Politics* (Rutgers University Press, 2004)

Rough Riders of the Coffee Bars', *The Times*, 8 June 1961

Mod

Anderson, Paul Smiler, *Mods: The New Religion: The Style and Music of the 1960s Mods* (Omnibus Press, 2013)

Hewitt, Paolo, *The Sharper Word: A Mod Anthology* (Helter Skelter Publishing, 2009)

'London: The Swinging City', *Time*, 15 April 1966

'Maximum Mod', Paolo Hewitt, *NME Originals Mod*, 1995

'Way Out Spoken: Young Mods have their Say on the Scene', *Rave Magazine*, May 1964

Surfer

'Bleachies, Beachies and Blasters on a Summer-in at Waikiki', Dan

Jenkins, *Sports Illustrated*, 24 July 1967

'The Surfies of Sydney', Anthony J. Lukas, *New York Times*, 23 November 1963

Hippie

'Flower Children Invade San Francisco', *The Times*, 1 July 1967

Wolfe, Tom, *The Electric Kool-Aid Acid Test* (Black Swan, new edition, 1989)

Rudeboy

Black, Pauline, *Black by Design: A Two-Tone Memoir* (Profile Books. 2011)

'Rude boys: Shanty Town to Savile Row', Sean O'Hagan, *Observer*, 24 May 2014

Skinhead

Marshall, George, *Spirit of '69: A Skinhead Bible* (Dunoon, 1994)

Hip Hop

Chang, Jeff, *Can't Stop Won't Stop: A History of the Hip-Hop Generation* (Ebury Publishing, 2011)

'Living the Lo-Life, B-Boys Go Preppy', *The Face*, December 1992

'New problems Encountered by Resurgent Street Gangs', John Darnton, *New York Times*, 21 February 1972

'Rap Music, Brash and Swaggering, Enters Mainstream', Glenn Collins, *New York Times*, 29 August 1988

Northern Soul

Constantine, Elaine and Sweeney, Gareth, *Northern Soul: An Illustrated History* (Virgin Books, 2013)

Nowell, David, *Too Darn Soulful: The Story of Northern Soul* (Robson Books Ltd. 1999)

Disco

Haden-Guest, Anthony, *The Last Party: Studio 54, Disco, and the Culture of the Night* (It Books, 2009)

'Tribal Rites of the New Saturday Night', Nik Cohn, *New York Magazine*, 7 June 1976

Punk

Bolton, Andrew, *Punk: Chaos to Couture* (Yale University Press, 2013)

'The Future Isn't What It Used to Be', Angus MacKinnon, *NME*, 13 September 1980

'Post punk', Suzy Menkes, *The Times*, 24 Feb 1981

'A Report on the Sex Pistols', Charles M. Young, *Rolling Stone*, 20 October 1977

New Romantic

Kemp, Gary, *I Know This Much: From Soho to Spandau* (Fourth Estate, 2009)

Dave Rimmer, *New Romantics: The Look* (Omnibus, Second Edition, 2013)

Goth

Spooner, Catherine, *Contemporary Gothic* (Reaktion Books, 2006)

Steele, Valerie, *Gothic: Dark Glamour* (Yale University Press, 2008)

Acid House

'Acid House and the Dawn of a Rave New World', Luke Bainbridge, *Observer*, 23 February 2014

'The Birth of Rave', Emma Warren, *Observer*, 12 August 2007

Broughton, Frank, *Boy's Own, The Complete Fanzines 1986–1992* (Bread and Circuses, 2009)

'Ecstasy', *The Face*, October 1985

'The Grin Factor', Wayne Anthony, *Q Magazine*, October 1988

Hook, Peter, *The Hacienda: How Not to Run a Club* (Pocket Books, 2010)

'Wonderland UK', Gavin Hill, *The Face*, January 1993

Goa Trance

'Goa Gil Interview', *Mushroom Magazine*, 12 August 2015

'Is Goa Trance the New Acid House?', *i.D*, issue 146, 1995

'New Invader on the Dance Floor', Simon Reynolds, *New York Times*, 29 November 1998

Grunge

Callahan, Maureen, *Champagne Supernovas: Kate Moss, Marc Jacobs, Alexander McQueen, and the 90s Renegades Who Remade Fashion* (Simon & Schuster UK, 2015)

'Grunge on the Catwalk', *The Face*, January 1993

Yarm, Mark, *Everybody Loves Our Town: A History of Grunge* (Faber and Faber, 2011)

Riot Grrrl

Gordon, Kim, *Girl in a Band* (Faber & Faber, 2015)

'Hole lotta love', Amy Raphael, *The Face*, February 1993

Marcus, Sara, *Girls to the Front: The True Story of the Riot Grrrl Revolution* (Harper Perennial, 2010)

'Revolution, Girl Style', *Newsweek*, 22 November 1992

'Strange Love', Lynn Hirschberg, *Vanity Fair*, September 1992

Britpop

Harris, John, *The Last Party: Britpop, Blair and the Demise of English Rock* (Harper Perennial, 2010)

'A Shite Sports Car and a Punk Reincarnation', John Harris, *NME*, 10 April 1993

Wener, Louise, *Different for Girls: My True-life Adventures in Pop* (Ebury Press, 2010)

Emo

'Emotionally challenged', Michelle Kirsch, *The Times*, 6 July 2006

Greenwald, Andy, *Nothing Feels Good: Punk Rock, Teenagers, and Emo* (St Martin's Press, 2013)

'Russia Wages War on Emo Kids', Sean Michaels, *Guardian*, 21 July 2008

'Why No Child is Safe from the Sinister Cult of Emo', Tom Rawstorne, *Daily Mail*, 16 May 2008

Neo-rockabilly

'NaNa: LA Punk to its Roots', Steffie Nelson, *Los Angeles Times*, 5 April 2009

'Stray Cats', Richard Williams, *The Times*, 9 August 1980

Hipster

'Berlin Wail', Joe Cunningham, *New York Post*, 22 February 2003

Vogel, Kristofor R, *Perceptions of Subversions: The Formation of a Pop-subculture* (The University of Texas, 2013)

'What was the Hipster?', Mark Greif, *New York Magazine*, 24 October 2010

Steampunk

'Get into Steampunk', Mark Keenan, *The Times*, 7 August 2011

Gleason, Katherine, *Anatomy of Steampunk* (Race Point Publishing, 2013)

'Steampunk Fashion Heading for the Mainstream', Jake Ellison, *Seattle Post-Intelligencer*, 18 January 2013

Harajuku Style

'Demure v Dominatrix', Laura M. Holson, *New York Times*, 13 March 2005

'Fashion Fusion in Tokyo', Guy Trebay, *New York Times*, 27 October 2002

'Fashion: Tokyo Teen Spirit', Mark O'Flaherty, *The Sunday Times*, 9 January 2005

Sapeur

'The Beau Brummels of Brazzaville', Tom Downey, *Wall Street Journal*, 29 September 2011

'Cry Freedom', Nigel Williamson, *The Times*, 10 January 2004

'Dream and Drama: The Search for Elegance Amongst Congolese Youth', Didier Gondola, *African Studies Review*, vol. 42, no.1, April 1999

'In Congo, Fashion From a Suitcase', James Brooke, *New York Times*, 17 March 1988

'The New People', Adam Howe, *The Face*, April 1993

Kogal

'Those Naughty Teenage Girls: Japanese Kogals, Slang and Media Assessments', Laura Miller, *Journal of Linguistic Anthropology*, December 2004

Index

Page numbers in *italics* refer to illustrations

Picture credits

Alamy Stock Photo
(Everett Collection Historical) 15 top left, (Photos 12) 15 bottom, (Keystone Pictures USA) 45 top right, (Pictorial Press Ltd.) 70 left, (Alpha Historica) 77 top left, (Trinity Mirror/Mirrorpix) 98, (Alex Segre) 166 far right, (James Lange) 210, (Alan Dawson Photography) 223 top right

Corbis Images
(Hulton-Deutsch Collection) 15 top right, 136, (Bettmann) 16, 28, 31, 32, 39 bottom, 45 bottom, 109, (Lebrecht Music & Arts) 26 bottom far left, (AS400 DB) 47, (Mauro Condé Nast Archive) 89, 124, 131, 135, (Laura Levine) 111 top, (Michael Ochs) 111 bottom, (HEX) 112 bottom, (Alex Tehrani) 114, (ClassicStock) 127 right, (Carraro/Sygma) 177 top & bottom left, (Dora Handel/CORBIS OUTLINE) 178, (Brian Mitchell) 200, (Vince Streano) 202, (Pacific Press) 221, (Per-Anders Pettersson) 235 bottom, 241 bottom, (Héctor Mediavilla/PT/Splash/Splash New) 236–7, (Ashley Gilbertson/VII) 247

Getty Images
(AFP) 2, 233, 235 top, 239, 241 top, (Diverse Images/UIG) 5, (Iconic Archive) 12, (Fox Photos) 17, (Anthony Barboza) 22, 24 top, (Keystone-France) 23, (JP Jazz Archive) 24 bottom, (Anthony Potter Collection) 33, (Archive Photos) 34 far left, (FPG) 36, (David E. Scherman) 39 left, (Peter Stackpole) 39 right, (Maurice Ambler) 42, (Fred W. McDarrah)

45 top left, (Joseph McKeown) 48, 55 left, (Popperfoto) 51, 70 right, 77 bottom, (Hulton Archive) 53, (Evening Standard) 55 right, 132, (Loomis Dean) 58–9, (Michael Ochs Archives) 61, 62, 80 bottom, 84, (New York Daily News Archive) 64 bottom, (Universal Images Group) 66, 95 left, 153, 155, 158, 163 bottom, 167, (Richard Frieman-Phelps) 68, (Jeremy Fletcher) 73, (Tom Kelley Archive) 74, (The Enthusiast Network) 77 top right, (Walter Iooss Jr.) 79, (Co Rentmeester) 80 top, (Lambert) 85 left, (John Dominis) 85 right, (Chris Ware) 93, (Virginia Turbett) 97, 103, 144 bottom, 149 bottom, 206 top, (Terrence Spencer) 101 top, (Caroline Greville-Morris) 104, (PYMCA) 106, 115, 188, 196, 197, 199, 205, 208, 212, 214, 215, 229, (Mick Gold) 120, 123 bottom left & right, (Tim Graham) 127 left, (Waring Abbott) 128, (Bob Olsen) 129, (Jack Garofalo) 137, (Brian Cooke) 138 top, (Michael Putland) 150, (Keystone) 154, (Pat Lyttle) 159, (Therese Frare) 174, (Ebet Roberts) 180, (Mick Hutson) 182, 191 right, (Steve Eichner) 183, (Kevin Cummins) 187, (Jessica Hromas) 206 bottom, (Pedro Gonzalez/CON) 207, (Adam Berry) 220, (Rachel Murray) 223 top left, (Jonathan Siegel) 245, 246 bottom

Kira/TokyoFashion.com
Cover, 224, 227, 228, 242

Mirrorpix
9, 50, 69, 87, 116, 123 top, 141, 142

PYMCA
Back cover, 90, 94

Rex/Shutterstock
(Ted Polhemus/PYMCA) 3,
102, 147, 149 top, 173 right, (Everett Collection) 19, (Nara Archives) 20, (Roger-Viollet) 41, (Frank Monaco) 56, 64 top, (David Graves) 82, (Rex Shutterstock) 86, (Local World) 95 right, (Stefano Archetti) 101 bottom, (Andre Csillag) 112 top, (ITV) 118–19, (Nils Jorgensen) 138 bottom, (Paul Hartnett/PYMCA) 140, (Sheila Rock) 144 top, (David Swindells/ PYMCA) 160, 164, 173 left, (Peter J Walsh / PYMCA) 165, (SIPA PRESS) 170 top, (Ralph L. Blair/ PYMCA) 191 left, (Sutton-Hibbert) 193, (Francisca Pinochet / PYMCA) 194, (Dosfotos/PYMCA) 213, (Tim Coleman) 223 bottom, (Top Photo Corporation) 230

Shutterstock
(PRILL) 18 left, (Ambient Ideas) 18 right, (Gordana Sermek) 26 top left, (Tei Sinthip) 26 top right, (Balefire, schankz) 34 centre, (S_ Photo) 34 right, (melissa held) 40 right, (Marina Tatarenko) 46 left, (Light and Dark Studio) 54 left, (NDT) 54 right, (Morozova Oxana) 65 centre, (dora modly-paris) 65 right, (trotalo) 72 left, (wolfman57) 72 centre, (Svetlana Prikhnenko) 72 right, (Shutterstock) 81 left & right, (William Perugini) 88 left, (Visun Khankasem) 88 centre, (benntennsann) 88 right, (John Abbate) 96 left, (popular business) 96 right, (Ariene Studio) 105 left, (joppo) 105 right, (Radu Bercan) 113 left, (Lenscap Photography) 113 centre, (A_Lesik) 113 right, (Ubonwan Poonpracha) 122 left, (aceshot1) 130 left, (Ortis) 130 right, (Claudio Divizia) 139 left, (Bayanova Svetlana) 139 centre, (Wanda Anthony) 139 right, (Everett Historical) 148 left, (Gemenacom) 148 right, (Bahadir Yeniceri) 156, (Maly
Designer) 157 left, (Timof) 157 centre, (FashionStock.com) 157 right, (wacomka) 166 left, (Lola Tsvetaeva) 166 centre, (P-fotography) 172 left, (nchlsft) 172 right, (aboikis) 179 left, (Tomnamon) 179 right, (iofoto) 186 right, (Sergey Goryachev) 192 right, (APaterson) 201 left, (nimon) 201 centre, (Richard Laschon) 201 right, (rvvlada) 209 left, (daizuoxin) 209 right, (mtlapcevic) 216 left, (canonzoom) 216 right, (pio3) 217, (Tinxi) 218, (Lupirro) 222 right, (Zoltan Kiraly) 231 left, (Shchipkova Elena) 231 centre, (s duffett) 231 right, (rui vale sousa) 241 left, (Shutter-Man) 241 right, (Takamex) 246 left, (aniad) 246 centre

Topfoto
27, (Ken Russell) 52

Caroline Young
60, 190

Sarah Young
168, 170 bottom left & right

Reuters
(Henry Romero) 35

FRONT COVER Style bloggers Francis Lola and Ellen V Lora, Harajuku, 2015
BACK COVER Rudeboy twins Chuka and Dubem, London, 1981
PAGE 2 Sapeur style, Kinshasa, 2014 PAGE 3 1980s London street style

Frances Lincoln Limited
A subsidiary of Quarto Publishing Group UK
74–77 White Lion Street, London N1 9PF

Style Tribes: The Fashion of Subcultures

First Frances Lincoln edition 2016

A catalogue record for this book is available from the British Library.

978-0-7112-3751-3

Printed and bound in China

1 2 3 4 5 6 7 8 9

Quarto is the authority on a wide range of topics.

Quarto educates, entertains and enriches the lives of
our readers – enthusiasts and lovers of hands-on living.

www.QuartoKnows.com